CALIFORNIA WINE COUNTRY

Bed & Breakfast
Cookbook and
Travel Guide

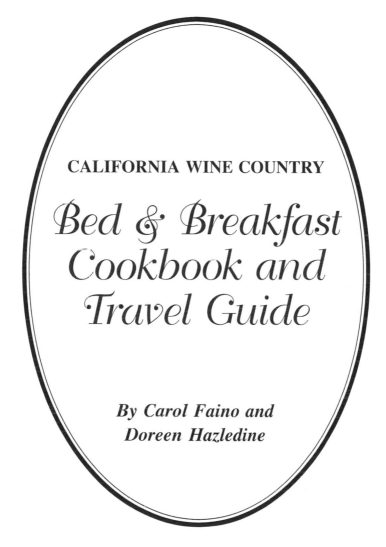

CALIFORNIA WINE COUNTRY

Bed & Breakfast Cookbook and Travel Guide

By Carol Faino and Doreen Hazledine

RUTLEDGE HILL PRESS®
Nashville, Tennessee

A Division of Thomas Nelson, Inc.
www.ThomasNelson.com

Published by Rutledge Hill Press, a division of Thomas Nelson, Inc., P.O. Box 141000, Nashville, Tennessee 37214.

Cover design by Ole Sykes, Sykes Design Graphics, Estes Park, Colorado.
Cover photo by Kevin Kester, Los Gatos, California.
Front cover location: Auberge du Soleil, Rutherford, California.
Author photo by Katrina Brown, Expressions Photography, Littleton, Colorado.
California map by Ole Sykes, Estes Park, Colorado.

The recipes chosen for inclusion are favorites of the inns and are not claimed to be original. Although the authors did not personally visit every inn, each recipe was home-kitchen tested, taste-tested, and edited for clarity.

Library of Congress Cataloging-in-Publication Data

Faino, Carol.
 California wine country : bed & breakfast cookbook and travel guide /
 by Carol Faino and Doreen Hazledine.
  p. cm.
 ISBN 1-55853-978-6
 1. Breakfasts. 2. Bed and breakfast accommocations—California—Guidebooks.
I. Hazledine, Doreen, 1948–   . II. Title.
 TX733.F35 2001
 641.5′2—dc21   2001006002

Printed in China
01 02 03 04 05 — 5 4 3 2 1

TO
my twin brother,
Duane Kaitfors,
*whose vision, love,
and steadfast support
made this book
possible.*

—*Doreen Kaitfors Hazledine*

Contents

Acknowledgments

Creating a book was a work involving many people. We owe a great deal of gratitude to the following friends and family members for their support, inspiration, time, and talents: Duane Kaitfors, Cynthia Kaitfors, Flora Van Deelen, Linda Faino, Terri Hulett, Doris Anderson, Morgan Anderson, Gordon McCollum, Joan Pasco, Ole Sykes, Margaret McCollum, Harold McCollum, Judy Cochran, Erin Faino, Jeanie Rienhardt, Krista Flock, and Gail and Rick Tysdal, who provided the impetus for the motorcycle symbol.

We greatly appreciate Larry Stone and Geoff Stone for making a beautiful book and Meg Ruley for believing in the project. A warm heartfelt thanks to our agent, Annelise Robey.

We are indebted to our dear friend, Doris Anderson, and to her husband, Morgan, whose indomitable and joyful spirit brightened our lives.

A special thank you to the California wine country bed and breakfast owners, innkeepers, and chefs who generously shared their recipes, artwork, enthusiasm, and encouragement.

We want to express our love and heartfelt thanks to our parents, Nan and Lawrence Kaitfors and Margaret and Harold McCollum; our husbands, Don Hazledine and Rod Faino; and children, Kyle, Erin, and Ryan Faino for their continuous support and encouragement.

Symbols' Key

   Covered parking available for motorcycles

   Smoking is prohibited

designated areas   Smoking permitted in designated areas

   Handicapped accessible

Can accommodate special dietary needs

Introduction

Let us open the door to your California wine country dream!

Sprinkled among the lush rolling hills and manicured vineyards of California's magical wine country are unique destinations that will delight all your senses. If you are ready to be pampered by your hosts, enlightened by their knowledge of local history and attractions, and stimulated by conversations with fellow travelers, then browse through our book and choose a bed and breakfast or country inn that is perfect for you.

With careful planning, you can experience a fun and enriching adventure and return home with memories that will last a lifetime. You can also create unforgettable breakfast feasts, appetizing luncheon and dinner entrées, and tempting desserts by preparing the many mouth-watering recipes that have received rave reviews from the bed and breakfast guests.

Due to the numerous requests by current owners of our *Colorado Bed & Breakfast Cookbook* and the *Washington State Bed & Breakfast Cookbook,* we have added symbols to indicate an inn's handicapped accessibility, motorcyle friendliness (secure parking), smoking restrictions, and ability to prepare menus to accommodate special dietary needs.

Whether you choose to awaken to the peaceful lull of the enchanting vineyards or the sound of waves breaking against the rocky coastline, the *California Wine Country Bed & Breakfast Cookbook and Travel Guide* will open the door to your California wine country dream.

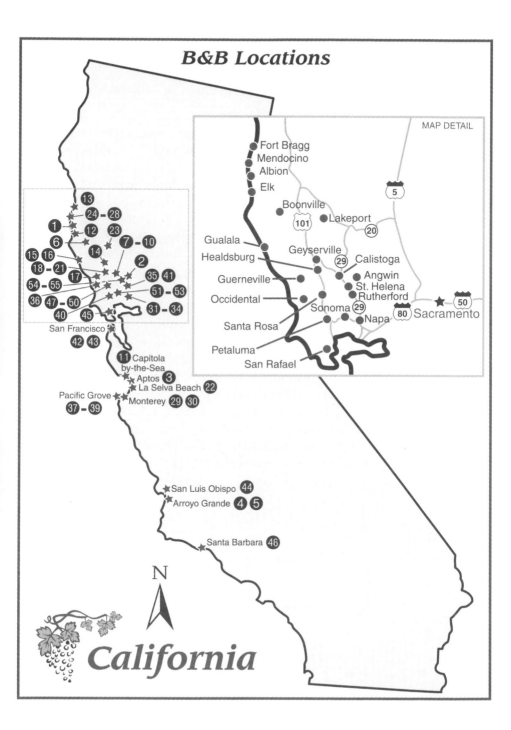

B&B Locations

MAP DETAIL

Fort Bragg
Mendocino
Albion
Elk
Boonville
Lakeport
Gualala
Geyserville
Calistoga
Healdsburg
Angwin
Guerneville
St. Helena
Rutherford
Occidental
Sonoma
Santa Rosa
Napa
Sacramento
Petaluma
San Rafael

San Francisco
Capitola
by-the-Sea
Aptos
La Selva Beach
Pacific Grove
Monterey

San Luis Obispo
Arroyo Grande

Santa Barbara

N

California

List of Inns and Towns (or Locations)

Beazley House Pineapple Bread

Blueberry Orange Bread

Cinnamon Bran Muffins

Cranberry Orange Muffins

Fresh Berry Muffins

Glazed Orange Chocolate Chip Muffins

Mandarin Orange Dried Cranberry
  Muffins

Michael's Organic Strawberry Bread

Onion Bread

Peach & Golden Raisin Muffins

Pecan Muffins with Strawberry Jam

Rosemary's Rosemary-Garlic Bread

Sally's Hawaiian Bread

Sherry Poppy Seed Bread

Breads
&
Muffins

Beazley House

T he Beazley House bed and breakfast sits on half an acre of lovely manicured lawns and gardens. Elegant yet comfortable, this welcome wine country retreat features large and individually decorated guest rooms, beautiful antiques, and private spas.

The bountiful breakfast buffet includes fresh-baked muffins, crustless quiche, a variety of fresh fruits with yogurt, orange juice, a selection of teas, and steaming coffee.

INNKEEPERS: *Jim & Carol Beazley*
ADDRESS: *1910 First Street*
Napa, CA 94559
TELEPHONE: *(707) 257-1649*
E-MAIL: *innkeeper@beazleyhouse.com*
WEBSITE: *www.beazleyhouse.com*
ROOMS: *11 Rooms; All with private baths*
ANIMALS: *Prohibited; Resident cat; Two resident dogs*

"Napa's first bed and breakfast, and it's still the best . . . you'll sense the hospitality as you stroll the walk past verdant lawns and bright flowers . . ."
—*The Annual Directory of American Bed and Breakfasts*

Beazley House
Pineapple Bread

Makes 3 loaves.

This low-fat pineapple bread contains very little oil, but is moist, nonetheless, with the addition of applesauce. To keep the bread fresh, wrap it tightly, and freeze what you do not use right away.

2 cups sugar
2 tablespoons canola oil
3 eggs
2 teaspoons vanilla extract
1 (20-ounce) can crushed pineapple (do not drain)
1 cup unsweetened applesauce
2½ plus 2 cups unbleached flour
3 teaspoons baking soda
2 teaspoons baking powder
1 cup low-fat buttermilk
1 tablespoon cinnamon

Preheat the oven to 325°F. Coat three 9x5-inch loaf pans with nonstick cooking spray. In a very large bowl, beat together the sugar, oil, eggs, and vanilla extract. Stir in the undrained pineapple and applesauce. In a medium bowl, sift together the 2½ cups of flour, baking soda, and baking powder. Add the dry mixture to the egg mixture. Mix until smooth. Add the buttermilk and stir. In a medium bowl, sift together the additional 2 cups flour and cinnamon. Add the flour/cinnamon mixture to the batter; stir until combined. Divide the batter evenly into the three loaf pans, filling each about two-thirds full. Bake for 45 minutes or until a toothpick inserted comes out clean. Let the bread cool in the pans on a wire rack for about 10 minutes. Loosen the edges of the bread, and turn out onto a wire rack to finish cooling. Serve the bread warm or at room temperature.

Melitta Station Inn

Originally built in the late 1800s, the Melitta Station Inn served as a country store and post office, rail depot, antique store, and a family home before it was lovingly converted into a bed and breakfast inn. Located in the heart of Sonoma County, the Melitta Station Inn is minutes from award-winning wineries. The comfortable rooms are tastefully furnished with distinct antiques and country collectibles.

Local points of interest include the picturesque town of Sonoma with its restored mission and Town Square, Jack London's State Historic Park and museum and the ruins of the fabled Wolf House.

An ample country breakfast is served each morning either in the sitting room or on the balcony. In the evening, guests enjoy wine and other refreshments before dining at local restaurants.

INNKEEPERS:	*Diane Crandon & Vic Amstadter*
ADDRESS:	*5850 Melitta Road*
	Santa Rosa, CA 95409
TELEPHONE:	*(707) 538-7712; (800) 504-3099*
E-MAIL:	*melittasta@aol.com*
WEBSITE:	*www.melittastationinn.com*
ROOMS:	*5 Rooms; 1 Suite; Rooms have private bathrooms; (Suite has two rooms, shared bathroom)*
CHILDREN:	*Children over the age of 12 are welcome; Younger children with prior arrangements*
ANIMALS:	*Prohibited*

Blueberry Orange Bread

Makes 1 loaf.

Easy, quick, and very good.

2 cups all-purpose flour
1 cup sugar
¼ teaspoon baking soda
1 teaspoon baking powder
½ teaspoon salt
1 egg, well beaten
2 tablespoons butter, melted
1 tablespoon grated orange (or lemon) peel (zest)
¾ cup orange juice
1 cup blueberries
2 tablespoons honey
2 tablespoons orange juice

Preheat the oven to 350°F. Grease a 9x5-inch loaf pan. In a large bowl, sift together the flour, sugar, baking soda, baking powder, and salt. Make a well in the center of the dry ingredients. In a medium bowl, combine the egg, melted butter, orange (or lemon) peel, and orange juice. Add the wet mixture all at once to the dry mixture. Stir just until moistened. Gently fold in the blueberries. Spoon batter into the prepared pan. Bake for 50 to 60 minutes, or until a wooden toothpick inserted near the center of the bread comes out clean. Cool in the pan on a wire rack for about 10 minutes. Remove the bread from the pan, and set the loaf on the wire rack. In a very small bowl, combine the honey with the orange juice. Using a pastry brush, glaze the loaf with the honey/orange juice mixture.

Cinnamon Bran Muffins

Makes approximately 48 muffins.

This is a large recipe, but the batter can be kept refrigerated in a covered container for several weeks. It's convenient and easy to bake only the number of muffins needed—in the morning, afternoon, or evening—whenever a fresh baked, delicious, and healthful treat is desired.

1 (17.7-ounce) box (5½ cups) bran buds
2 cups boiling water
3 cups sugar
4 eggs, beaten
1 cup oil
5 cups all-purpose flour
1½ teaspoons cinnamon
1½ tablespoons baking soda
2 teaspoons salt
1 tablespoon grated orange peel (zest)
2 cups raisins
4 cups (1 quart) buttermilk
Cinnamon sugar (1 cup sugar plus 1 teaspoon cinnamon)
Honey or apple butter, for serving

In a very large bowl, mix the bran buds and boiling water; let stand for 10 minutes. In a large bowl, mix together the sugar, eggs, and oil; add to the soaked bran buds. In another bowl, sift together the flour, cinnamon, baking soda, and salt. Stir in the orange zest and raisins. Add the flour mixture to the bran mixture alternately with the buttermilk. Stir until combined. To bake muffins, preheat the oven to 350°F. Coat the muffin cups (for the number of muffins desired) with nonstick cooking spray. Fill the cups with batter two-thirds full. Sprinkle with the cinnamon sugar mixture. Bake for 15 to 20 minutes (refrigerated batter will take about 5 to 10 minutes longer), or until a tester comes out clean. Serve the muffins warm with honey or apple butter.

(For inn information see page 126)

Cranberry Orange Muffins

Makes 30 muffins.

Plan ahead if you are using dried cranberries, because they need to soak overnight in the juice from the mandarin oranges.

5 cups all-purpose flour
1⅔ cups sugar
2 tablespoons baking powder
1 teaspoon salt
¾ cup (1½ sticks) butter, melted
7 eggs
1⅔ cups orange juice
1 tablespoon grated orange peel (zest)
2 cups fresh cranberries or ¾ cup dried cranberries
1 (11-ounce) can mandarin oranges, drained (save juice for soaking
**   if using dried cranberries)**

Preheat the oven to 375°F. Coat the muffin cups with nonstick cooking spray. In a very large bowl, combine the flour, sugar, baking powder, and salt. Make a well in the center of the dry ingredients. In a large bowl, whisk together the melted butter and eggs. Stir in the orange juice and orange peel. Add the liquid ingredients to the dry mixture, and stir just until moistened. Gently fold in the fresh cranberries (cut in half), or drained dried cranberries and mandarin oranges (cut in half). Bake the muffins for 15 to 20 minutes, or until the tops of the muffins are lightly browned. Place the muffin pans on a wire rack to cool.

(For inn information see page 126)

Union Street Inn

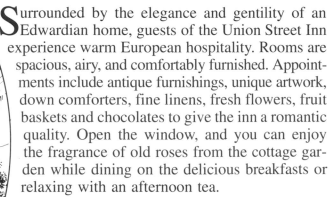

Surrounded by the elegance and gentility of an Edwardian home, guests of the Union Street Inn experience warm European hospitality. Rooms are spacious, airy, and comfortably furnished. Appointments include antique furnishings, unique artwork, down comforters, fine linens, fresh flowers, fruit baskets and chocolates to give the inn a romantic quality. Open the window, and you can enjoy the fragrance of old roses from the cottage garden while dining on the delicious breakfasts or relaxing with an afternoon tea.

Nestled in one of San Francisco's fashionable shopping and dining areas, the surroundings have a charming, international flavor. Fisherman's Wharf, Ghirardelli Square, Pier 39, the Golden Gate Bridge, and downtown San Francisco are minutes away.

INNKEEPER:	*Jane Bertorelli*
ADDRESS:	*2229 Union Street*
	San Francisco, CA 94123
TELEPHONE:	*(415) 346-0424*
E-MAIL:	*Not available*
WEBSITE:	*www.unionstreetinn.com*
ROOMS:	*6 Rooms; All with private baths*
CHILDREN:	*Welcome*
ANIMALS:	*Prohibited; Resident cat and dog*

Fresh Berry Muffins

Makes 12 large or 18 standard-size muffins.

Blueberries or raspberries may be substituted for the strawberries in these fruity gems. These muffins are best served hot out of the oven.

3 cups all-purpose flour
⅔ cup sugar
1 teaspoon baking soda
½ teaspoon baking powder
1 teaspoon salt
1½ cups strawberries, coarsely chopped
2 eggs, beaten
¼ cup cooking oil
1 teaspoon almond extract
Buttermilk (you will need about 1⅓ cups, see directions below)

Preheat the oven to 375°F. Grease the cups of the muffin pans. In a large bowl, combine the flour, sugar, baking soda, baking powder, and salt. Add strawberries (or berries of choice), and toss gently to coat. Make a well in the center of the dry mixture. In a 3-cup capacity measuring cup or bowl, combine the eggs, oil, and almond extract. Add the buttermilk until the total amount of liquid mixture measures 2⅛ cups. Stir the wet mixture into the dry ingredients; combine just until moistened. Do not overmix. Spoon the batter into the prepared pans, filling each cup two-thirds full. Bake for 20 to 25 minutes for large muffins, or approximately 18 minutes for standard-size muffins, or until the muffins are lightly browned. Let the muffins cool in pans on a wire rack for 2 to 3 minutes. Carefully remove the muffins and serve.

Carol's Corner
When spooning the batter into the muffin cups, try to avoid placing pieces of strawberry directly on the bottom of the muffin cups (spoon a little plain batter in first), or you will end up with "holes" on the bottom of your baked muffins. For a special touch, brush the baked muffin tops with melted butter and sprinkle with sugar.

Agate Cove Inn

Perched on a bluff above the Pacific Ocean, the Agate Cove Inn delivers breathtaking ocean views. Surrounded by two acres of beautiful gardens framed by one-hundred-year-old cypress trees, the blue-and-white trimmed cottages have rooms with ocean or garden views, and most of them come with fireplaces and decks. Agate Cove provides unforgettable experiences to its guests as the perfect setting for weddings, anniversary and birthday celebrations, holidays, or just a relaxing getaway.

The scrumptious country breakfast features fresh-baked muffins, award-winning bread and cooked-to-order entrées that are accompanied by baked apples, poached pears, homemade applesauce, and fresh fruit bowls.

INNKEEPERS:	*Dennis & Nancy Freeze*
ADDRESS:	*11201 Lansing Street*
	Mendocino, CA 95460
TELEPHONE:	*(707) 937-0551; (800) 527-3111*
E-MAIL:	*reservations@agatecove.com*
WEBSITE:	*www.agatecove.com*
ROOMS:	*2 Rooms; 8 Cottages; All with private baths*
CHILDREN:	*Children over the age of 12 are welcome*
ANIMALS:	*Prohibited; Resident dog*

Glazed Orange Chocolate Chip Muffins

Makes 12 muffins.

Muffins:

2 cups all-purpose flour
¾ cup sugar
¾ teaspoon baking soda
1 teaspoon baking powder
¼ teaspoon salt
1 cup chocolate chips
8 ounces vanilla yogurt

⅓ cup canola oil
1 egg
2 teaspoons orange extract
½ cup mandarin oranges,
  drained and coarsely chopped
Zest from 2 navel oranges,
  finely chopped

Preheat the oven to 350°F. Grease the muffin cups. In a large bowl, combine the flour, sugar, baking soda, baking powder, salt, and chocolate chips. In a medium bowl, combine the yogurt, oil, egg, orange extract, oranges, and orange zest. Add the wet ingredients to the dry mixture; stir just until moistened. Spoon the batter into muffin cups, filling each two-thirds full. Bake the muffins for 25 to 30 minutes. Cool in the pans on a wire rack for 5 to 10 minutes. Remove the muffins from the pans, and brush with Orange Glaze. (Prepare the glaze while the muffins are baking.)

Orange Glaze:
Makes enough glaze for 2 batches of muffins.

1¼ cups orange marmalade
½ cup sugar
½ cup water

In a saucepan, combine the marmalade, sugar, and water. Bring the mixture to a rapid boil, stirring constantly. Lower the heat, but keep the mixture boiling, stirring occasionally, until the mixture has reduced significantly (about 20 minutes). The mixture should form a lump when a small amount is dropped into cold water. Remove the pan from the heat, and strain the glaze, discarding the solids. Using a pastry brush, glaze the muffins immediately, because the glaze starts to harden as it cools down. The glaze stays somewhat tacky on the muffins and is "finger-lickin' good." Store the leftover glaze at room temperature. To reuse, add a small amount of water and heat to boiling.

Gatehouse Inn

O riginally constructed in 1884 as a summer residence for Senator Langford, the Gatehouse Inn is a charming Italianate Victorian. Senator Langford, in an act of civil disobedience, chopped down the gate to Pacific Grove, a Methodist retreat, hence the name Gatehouse Inn. Today there are nine romantic guest rooms. In the evening look for a chocolate on your pillow.

Situated in Pacific Grove on the scenic Monterey Peninsula, you can take a short walk to the town of Pacific Grove or bicycle along the edge of the bay or take a short drive to Carmel, winding your way back along the Seventeen-Mile Drive.

A gourmet breakfast of fresh fruit, homemade breads and muffins, and steaming mugs of our special blends of coffee and tea is served every morning. In the afternoon more home-cooked treats are served with wine.

INNKEEPER:	*Ruby Rustan*
ADDRESS:	*225 Central Avenue*
	Pacific Grove, CA 93950
TELEPHONE:	*(831) 649-8436; (800) 753-1881*
E-MAIL:	*lew@sueandlewinns.com*
WEBSITE:	*www.sueandlewinns.com*
ROOMS:	*9 Rooms; All with private baths*
CHILDREN:	*Children over the age of 7 are welcome*
ANIMALS:	*Prohibited*

designated areas

Mandarin Orange Dried Cranberry Muffins

Makes 18 muffins.

These flavorful muffins are wonderful served hot from the oven.

2¾ cups all-purpose flour
¾ cup packed brown sugar
¾ cup sugar
1 teaspoon baking soda
1 teaspoon baking powder
½ teaspoon salt
⅓ cup butter, melted and cooled
2 eggs
¾ cup buttermilk
1 tablespoon vanilla extract
¾ teaspoon lemon extract
¾ teaspoon orange extract
1 (11-ounce) can mandarin oranges, drained and cut in half
¾ cup dried cranberries
About 3 tablespoons sugar, for topping

Preheat the oven to 350°F. Grease the muffin cups (2¾x1¼-inch deep), or line with paper baking cups. In a large bowl, combine the first 6 dry ingredients. Make a well in the center of the dry mixture. In a medium bowl, whisk together the butter, eggs, buttermilk, and extracts. Add the wet ingredients to the dry ingredients; mix just until moistened. Gently fold in the mandarin oranges and cranberries. Spoon the batter into the muffin cups, filling each three-fourths full. Sprinkle the top of each muffin generously with sugar (about ½ teaspoon each). Bake the muffins for 20 to 24 minutes, or until the tops of the muffins are lightly browned. Cool the muffin pans on a wire rack for about 5 minutes. Gently remove the muffins from the pans and serve.

Glenborough Inn

Surrounded by gardens on a quiet, tree-lined street, the Glenborough Inn is the perfect romantic getaway. Located three blocks from downtown Santa Barbara and fourteen blocks from the seashore, guest accommodations at this cozy bed and breakfast include Jacuzzis, decks, and independent sitting areas. Most rooms have private entrances, fireplaces, in-room coffee service and mini-refrigerators. Amenities include fluffy bath and spa towels, robes, fresh flowers, and an enclosed garden hot tub. Specialty items available include spa body wraps, massages, champagne, wine, flowers, special occasion cakes and gift certificates.

The daily morning routine at the Glenborough Inn includes a delicious hot gourmet breakfast delivered to each guest room or suite. Guests select a specified time and dine at their pleasure. Privacy is highly respected at this romantic hideaway. Guests need never leave their chambers.

INNKEEPERS:	*Annya, Lacie, Jessica, John; Marlies, Owner*
ADDRESS:	*1327 Bath Street*
	Santa Barbara, CA 93101
TELEPHONE:	*(805) 966-0589; (888) 966-0589*
E-MAIL:	*glenboro@silcom.com*
WEBSITE:	*www.glenboroughinn.com*
ROOMS:	*18 Rooms; 6 Suites; 2 Cottages; Private baths*
CHILDREN:	*Welcome*
ANIMALS:	*Prohibited*

designated areas

Michael's Organic Strawberry Bread

Makes 2 loaves.

Substitution of non-organic ingredients, including frozen fruit, may be made.

3 cups organic wheat flour
1 teaspoon baking soda
1 teaspoon salt
1 tablespoon cinnamon
2 cups sugar
4 eggs, beaten
1½ cups canola oil
2 cups small, whole strawberries, washed, stems removed
1 cup diced strawberries
1 cup organic chopped pecans, optional
Butter, for serving
Fresh fruit preserves, for serving

Preheat the oven to 325°F. Grease, or coat with nonstick cooking spray, two loaf pans (9x5 inches). In a large bowl, sift together the 5 dry ingredients. In a medium bowl, mix the eggs and oil together for 1 minute. Gently add the whole strawberries to the egg mixture. Carefully add the egg/strawberry mixture to the dry ingredients; avoid crushing the berries. Gently fold in the diced strawberries, and add the pecans, if desired. Spoon the batter into prepared pans. Bake for 60 to 75 minutes, or until a knife inserted in the center comes out clean. Cool on a wire rack for about 15 minutes before removing bread. Serve with butter and fresh fruit preserves.

Blue Violet Mansion

Located in Napa's historic district on a quiet street in Old Town Napa, the Blue Violet Mansion is a graceful Queen Anne Victorian residence that has been lovingly restored by its innkeepers. Evidence of Emanuel Manasse's embossed leather still adorns the main staircase and second-floor foyer. Situated on an acre of private gardens, this historic home is within walking distance of shops and restaurants. Hot air balloon trips are available before breakfast. The famous Napa Valley Wine Train is ten blocks away.

Guest accommodations include gas-burning fireplaces, spas for two, whirlpool baths, designer bathrobes, voice mail, and modem outlets.

A full two-course French country breakfast is served each morning. The daily changing menu includes pastries, quiches, pancakes, and much more.

INNKEEPERS: *Bob & Kathy Morris; Robert Stine, GM*
ADDRESS: *443 Brown Street*
Napa, CA 94559
TELEPHONE: *(707) 253-2583; (800) 959-2583*
E-MAIL: *bviolet@napanet.net*
WEBSITE: *www.bluevioletmansion.com*
ROOMS: *17 Rooms; All with private baths*
CHILDREN: *Welcome*
ANIMALS: *Prohibited*

designated areas

Onion Bread

Makes about 12 servings.

This flavorful bread with a custard-like topping can be served as an appetizer or as an accompaniment with lunch or dinner. For a milder and sweeter onion flavor, try using Vidalia or Walla Walla onions when they are in season.

6 tablespoons butter
4 large yellow onions, peeled and thinly sliced
3 eggs
2 cups sour cream
½ teaspoon salt
14 ounces basic bread dough (or use a 16-ounce loaf of frozen bread
    dough, thawed)
1 tablespoon poppy seeds

Preheat the oven to 350°F. Grease a 13x9-inch baking pan. In a large sauté pan, melt the butter. Add the onions and sauté until they are transparent and tender. In a large bowl, beat the eggs and combine with the sour cream and salt. Add the sautéed onions (including the butter) to the egg/sour cream mixture. Mix well. On a floured surface, roll out the dough to a 15x11-inch rectangle. Line the prepared pan with the dough, turning the dough up 1 inch around the sides. Pour the onion/sour cream mixture over the dough, and sprinkle with the poppy seeds. Bake for 60 minutes, or until golden brown. Let the onion bread cool in the pan for about 10 minutes for easier cutting.

Old St. Angela Inn

Built as a country home in 1910, the Old St. Angela Inn was converted into a rectory, then a convent in 1920, and today it is an elegant inn, featuring New England-style hospitality at its best. Turn-of-the-century antiques, little Teddy bears, and other pleasantries provide a relaxing informal home away from home. Overlooking the beautiful Monterey Bay, this cozy bed and breakfast is only minutes from Old Cannery Row and the Monterey Bay Aquarium. The Pacific Ocean is a mere one hundred yards away. Walk to beaches, parks, museums, and famed Lover's Point. The innkeeper will assist guests with dinner reservations, tours, picnics, bike rides, and other special services.

A delicious breakfast is served in either the redwood and glass solarium that overlooks the garden or in the dining room with its ocean view.

INNKEEPERS: *Susan Kuslis & Lewis Shaefer*
ADDRESS: *321 Central Avenue*
Pacific Grove, CA 93950
TELEPHONE: *(800) 748-6306*
E-MAIL: *lew@sueandlewinns.com*
WEBSITE: *www.sueandlewinns.com*
ROOMS: *9 Rooms; All with private baths*
CHILDREN: *Children over the age of five are welcome*
ANIMALS: *Prohibited; Resident dog*

designated areas

Peach & Golden Raisin Muffins

Makes 12 muffins.

1 (15¼-ounce) can peach slices, drained
1 egg
¼ cup vegetable oil
1 teaspoon vanilla extract
¼ teaspoon almond extract
1 teaspoon grated orange peel (zest)
1 cup all-purpose flour
2 teaspoons baking powder
1 teaspoon cinnamon
1 cup rolled oats (old-fashioned or quick-cooking)
¾ cup packed brown sugar
½ cup golden raisins

Preheat the oven to 350°F. Grease 12 muffin cups (2¾x1¼ inches deep). Chop 2 peach slices. Purée the remaining peach slices (the purée should measure a scant cupful). In a medium bowl, beat the egg. Combine the egg with the peach purée, oil, vanilla and almond extracts, and the grated orange peel. In a large bowl, sift together the flour, baking powder, and cinnamon. Stir in the rolled oats and brown sugar. Make a well in the center of the dry ingredients. Add the wet mixture to the dry ingredients; stir just until moistened. Gently fold in the chopped peaches and golden raisins. Fill the prepared muffin cups about three-fourths full. Bake for 16 to 18 minutes, or until a toothpick inserted in the center comes out clean. Cool in the muffin cups on a wire rack for 5 minutes. Gently remove the muffins and serve warm.

Inn on Randolph

T he Inn on Randolph is the ideal location from which to explore the spectacular Napa Valley wine country. This beautifully restored historic property consists of an 1860 Victorian home and three 1930s cottages. Situated on one-half acre of landscaped grounds in Old Town Napa, guests enjoy the serenity of a quiet residential neighborhood close to shops and restaurants.

Amenities include fireplaces, whirlpool tubs, private decks, and bountiful breakfasts. Guests relax in the parlor, gather around the grand piano for an impromptu sing-along, or swing lazily in the garden hammock.

A bountiful Southern-style breakfast is served each morning.

INNKEEPER:	*Deborah Coffee*
ADDRESS:	*411 Randolph Street*
	Napa, CA 94559
TELEPHONE:	*(707) 257-2886; (800) 670-6886*
E-MAIL:	*Not available*
WEBSITE:	*www.innonrandolph.com*
ROOMS:	*5 Rooms; 3 Cottages; Private baths*
CHILDREN:	*Welcome*
ANIMALS:	*Prohibited; Resident cat*

  designated areas

Pecan Muffins
with Strawberry Jam

Makes 18 muffins.

For a special Valentine's Day treat, use heart-shaped muffin pans.

1½ cups all-purpose flour
½ cup sugar
1½ teaspoons baking powder
¼ teaspoon baking soda
¼ teaspoon salt
1 egg
1 cup sour cream
½ cup (1 stick) unsalted butter, melted
1 teaspoon vanilla
¼ cup pecans, toasted and chopped fine
½ cup (approximately) strawberry jam

Preheat the oven to 400°F. Lightly grease or butter muffin pans. In a medium bowl, combine the flour, sugar, baking powder, baking soda, and salt. Make a well in the center. In another medium bowl, combine the egg, sour cream, melted butter, and vanilla. Add the wet mixture, along with the pecans, to the dry ingredients. Stir just until blended; do not overmix. Spoon the batter into prepared muffin pans, filling the cups one-half full. With the back of a teaspoon, make a small well in the top of the batter in each cup. Spoon about one teaspoon of jam into each well. Bake for 12 to 15 minutes, or until the muffins are golden. Cool in pans on a wire rack for about 5 minutes. Remove from the muffin pans.

St. Orres Inn

Located on a sunny stretch of coastline that overlooks the Pacific Ocean, the St. Orres Inn sits on forty-two acres of amazing beauty. Reflecting a genuine love and respect for the land and its history, the owners have created the perfect getaway. Perched on the rise above a sheltered sandy cove, the St. Orres Inn has the appearance of a nineteenth-century Russian country house. This amazing structure was built with timbers salvaged from a one-hundred-year-old sawmill. One of the cabins, the Sequoia Cottage, offers an ocean view from its very private deck. The handcrafted, timber-frame interior boasts a sitting area with an inviting window seat and a wood-burning stove.

A full complimentary gourmet breakfast is served to each room. The innovative cuisine includes everything from appetizers such as goat cheese and smoked wild boar to dinner favorites like venison, pheasant, quail, and rack of lamb.

INNKEEPERS: *Rosemary Campiformio; Ted & Eric Black*
ADDRESS: *36601 Coast Highway 1*
Gualala, CA 95445
TELEPHONE: *(707) 884-3303*
E-MAIL: *rosemary@mcn.org*
WEBSITE: *www.saintorres.com*
ROOMS: *8 Rooms; 13 Cottages; Private & shared baths*
CHILDREN: *Welcome*
ANIMALS: *Prohibited*

designated areas

Rosemary's Rosemary-Garlic Bread

Makes 3 round loaves.

Bread:
1 package dry yeast
1 tablespoon sugar
1 cup warm water (105°–115°F.)
4 teaspoons finely chopped
   fresh rosemary leaves
8 tablespoons roasted garlic,
   mashed (you'll need to roast
   3 large bulbs to have enough
   for topping)
3 tablespoons olive oil

1 teaspoon salt
2 egg whites, room temperature
3 to 3½ cups bread flour

Topping:
1 teaspoon cornstarch
½ teaspoon salt
¼ cup water
3 tablespoons mashed, roasted
   garlic
1 to 2 tablespoons butter, melted

To make the bread, in a mixer fitted with a dough hook, combine the yeast, sugar, and water. Add the rosemary, 8 tablespoons roasted garlic, olive oil, salt, and egg whites. With the mixer running, add the flour a little at a time until it is incorporated and kneaded well. (Dough will be soft and sticky.) Dust your hands with flour and form the dough into a ball. Place the dough in a greased bowl, turning once to coat both sides with the oil. Cover the bowl with a clean towel, and let the dough rise until it doubles in size, about 40 minutes. Divide the risen dough into 3 equal parts; shape with your hands into rounds, each approximately ¾-inch thick. Place the rounds on a lightly greased baking sheet.

   To make the topping, combine the cornstarch, salt, water, and the 3 tablespoons roasted garlic. Brush the dough with topping, discarding any leftover liquid. Let the dough rise, uncovered, until double in size, about 30 minutes. Preheat the oven to 350°F. Bake for 25 minutes. Remove from the oven; brush the loaves with the butter. Place the bread back into the oven to finish baking, about 5 minutes longer, until golden brown. Serve warm, or cool the bread on a wire rack for later use.

Silver Rose Inn

Nestled on a peaceful twenty-acre estate, the Silver Rose Inn & Spa has the intimacy of a bed and breakfast inn and the elegance of a four-star resort. It is surrounded by natural beauty, from lush vineyards and majestic mountains to the splendor of the rose garden and the peaceful gurgling of the creek that meanders through the grounds. Located within minutes of Napa Valley's world-class wineries, restaurants, and shopping, the Silver Rose offers, in two separate inns, twenty spacious rooms. The Inn on the Knoll is the original inn and spa facility. The Inn in the Vineyard hosts an adjoining state-of-the-art conference center.

INNKEEPERS: *Derrick, J-Paul & Sally Dumont, Proprietors*
ADDRESS: *351 Rosedale Road*
Calistoga, CA 94515
TELEPHONE: *(707) 942-9581; (800) 995-9381*
E-MAIL: *silvrose@napanet.net*
WEBSITE: *www.silverrose.com*
ROOMS: *19 Rooms; 1 Suite; All with private baths*
CHILDREN: *Children over the age of 12 are welcome*
ANIMALS: *Prohibited; Resident cat*

designated areas

Sally's Hawaiian Bread

Makes 2 loaves.

Pineapple, coconut, and grated carrots combine beautifully in this flavorful and moist quick bread.

1 cup vegetable oil
2 cups sugar
3 eggs
2 teaspoons vanilla extract
2⅔ cups all-purpose flour
1 teaspoon salt (optional, if lower salt intake is desired)
1 teaspoon baking soda
1 teaspoon cinnamon
1 cup (or use a 15½-ounce can) drained crushed pineapple
1 cup shredded coconut
2 cups grated raw carrots

Preheat the oven to 350°F. Grease and flour two loaf pans (9x5 inches). In a large bowl, beat together the oil, sugar, and eggs. Add the vanilla. Sift together the flour, salt, baking soda, and cinnamon. Add the dry ingredients to the sugar/egg mixture. Gently stir in the drained pineapple, coconut, and carrots. Divide the batter between the two prepared loaf pans. Bake for 55 to 60 minutes, or until a wooden toothpick inserted near the center comes out clean. Cool in the pans on a wire rack for about 10 minutes. Remove the bread from the pans. This bread is good warm, but it slices better after it has cooled. Freezes well.

Note: Drain the pineapple before measuring it. If you wish to make only one loaf of bread, cut the recipe in half and use a drained, 8-ounce can of crushed pineapple.

Honor Mansion

Originally built in 1883, the Honor Mansion is shaded by a one-hundred-year-old magnolia tree. In 1994, Cathi and Steve Fowler renovated the entire building, converting it from a dark and discouraging old vestige into the crisp, elegant and magnificent Victorian it is today. From mints on pillows to a full gourmet breakfast, guests are pampered in this magical and remarkable bed and breakfast inn.

While enjoying this romantic getaway, guests appreciate the easy access to the more than 150 wineries in Sonoma Valley, Alexander Valley, Dry Creek Valley, and the Russian River Valley. Healdsburg's charming historic plaza is within walking distance.

Breakfast at the Honor Mansion is a culinary treat. Delectable entrées include caramel apple French toast and mansion eggs Benedict. Fresh juices, ground gourmet coffees, and a full assortment of teas and cocoas complement the morning entrée.

INNKEEPERS:	*Steve & Cathi Fowler*
ADDRESS:	*14891 Grove Street*
	Healdsburg, CA 95448
TELEPHONE:	*(707) 433-4277; (800) 554-4667*
E-MAIL:	*cathi@honormansion.com*
WEBSITE:	*www.honormansion.com*
ROOMS:	*5 Rooms; 4 Suites; All with private baths*
CHILDREN:	*Unsuitable*
ANIMALS:	*Prohibited*

Sherry Poppy Seed Bread

Makes 3 loaves or 1 large Bundt cake.

A perfect accompaniment to afternoon tea. Because this bread freezes well, it's effortless to serve a special treat to unexpected guests.

4 cups sifted cake flour
3 teaspoons baking powder
1 teaspoon salt
1 teaspoon nutmeg
¼ cup poppy seeds
1 (3.4-ounce) package instant vanilla pudding
1 cup (2 sticks) butter, room temperature
2 cups sugar
4 eggs
1 tablespoon vanilla extract
1⅓ cups milk, room temperature
¾ cup cream sherry

Preheat the oven to 350°F. Grease and flour 3 loaf pans (9x5 inches) or one large (12-cup) Bundt pan. In a large bowl, combine the cake flour, baking powder, salt, nutmeg, poppy seeds, and dry instant pudding. In another large bowl, combine the butter and sugar; beat vigorously. Add the eggs, one at a time, beating after each addition. Add the vanilla. Alternating among the three, gradually add the milk, sherry, and dry ingredients, mixing completely after each addition. When the batter is blended, beat vigorously for 30 seconds. Pour the batter into the prepared pan(s). Bake in the loaf pans for 45 minutes (or in the large Bundt pan for 55 to 60 minutes), or until a wooden toothpick comes out clean. Cool in the pan(s) for about 15 minutes on a wire rack. Remove the bread from the pan(s); cool completely on a wire rack.

Budapest Coffee Cake
Carol's Cranberry Scones
Cherry-Orange Scones
Date-Nut Coffee Cake Supreme
Oatmeal Scones
Orange-Scented Scones
Orange Scones
The General's Daughter Scones
Union Street Inn Scones
Yogurt Coffee Cake

Coffee Cakes & Scones

Ramekins

Located a few blocks from Sonoma's historical town plaza, Ramekins houses a world-class culinary school, a beautifully designed bed and breakfast inn, and a great hall and garden patio for special events. Classes at the culinary school last approximately three hours and include recipes, a generous sampling of all the dishes prepared in class, and delicious Sonoma Valley wines.

The beautifully decorated guest rooms are uniquely adorned with custom furnishings, four-poster beds, down comforters, original art, modem-ready telephones with voice mail, cable television, and oversized bathrooms.

A well-stocked Kitchen Shop is located on the ground floor and offers a vast assortment of cookbooks, chef's coats, cutlery, and kitchenware.

INNKEEPERS:	*Marilyn Piraino; Suzanne Bringham, Owner*
ADDRESS:	*450 West Spain Street*
	Sonoma, CA 95476
TELEPHONE:	*(707) 933-0452*
E-MAIL:	*bandb@ramekins.com*
WEBSITE:	*www.ramekins.com*
ROOMS:	*6 Rooms; All with private baths*
CHILDREN:	*Children over the age of 12 are welcome*
ANIMALS:	*Prohibited*

designated areas

Budapest Coffee Cake

Makes 18 individual-size Bundt cakes.

Batter:
1¼ cups butter, room
  temperature
2¼ cups sugar
1 tablespoon vanilla extract
5 eggs
4½ cups all-purpose flour
1 tablespoon baking powder
1 tablespoon baking soda
¾ teaspoon salt
3 cups sour cream

½ tablespoon cinnamon
½ cup chopped pecans

Glaze:
1 cup powdered sugar
½ teaspoon vanilla extract
4 to 6 tablespoons cream
¼ cup (approximately) chopped,
  toasted pecans, for topping

Streusel:
½ cup packed brown sugar
½ tablespoon unsweetened
  cocoa powder

Preheat the oven to 325°F. Grease and flour the Bundt pans. In a large bowl, cream together the butter, sugar and vanilla. Beat in the eggs, one at a time. Sift together the flour, baking powder, baking soda, and salt; add to the butter mixture in three parts, alternating with the sour cream.

To make the streusel, in a medium bowl, combine the brown sugar, cocoa powder, cinnamon, and pecans. Spoon the batter into the Bundt pans, alternating with the streusel (there will be three layers of batter and two layers of streusel). Try to keep the streusel in the middle and away from the edges of the pan. Bake approximately 20 to 25 minutes, or until the tops spring back when lightly touched. Remove from the oven; cool on a wire rack.

While the cake is cooling, make the glaze by combining in a small bowl the powdered sugar, vanilla, and enough cream to make drizzling consistency. When the cakes are cool, remove them from the pans, and drizzle the glaze over the top and sides. Sprinkle with the pecans.

Whitegate Inn

B uilt entirely from redwood in 1883, this lovely bed and breakfast was Mendocino's hospital in the late 1880s. Now, ancient cypress trees and colorful gardens surround the Whitegate Inn bed and breakfast. The décor is elegant, set off by striking antiques and fresh flowers. Located in the heart of Mendocino and surrounded by gorgeous gardens and panoramic views of the rugged Pacific Coast, the Whitegate Inn is a splendid example of classic, meticulously restored Victorian architecture. Rooms include fireplaces, televisions, and irresistibly comfy European feather beds.

Breakfast favorites include caramel apple French toast, pecan and date pancakes, and cheese soufflé.

INNKEEPERS:	*George & Carol Bechtloff*
ADDRESS:	*499 Howard Street*
	Mendocino, CA 95460
TELEPHONE:	*(800) 531-7282*
E-MAIL:	*staff@whitegateinn.com*
WEBSITE:	*www.whitegateinn.com*
ROOMS:	*6 Rooms; 1 Cottage; All with private baths*
CHILDREN:	*Welcome*
ANIMALS:	*Prohibited; Resident cat*

designated areas

Carol's Cranberry Scones

Makes 12 scones.

Carol Bechtloff, co-owner and innkeeper (along with her husband George) at Whitegate Inn, shares her wonderful scone recipe that combines cranberries with the complementary taste of lemon. The aroma during baking has been known to arouse even the sleepiest of guests.

3 cups all-purpose flour
½ cup sugar
¼ teaspoon salt
1 tablespoon baking powder
¾ cup (1½ sticks) unsalted butter, chilled and cut into pieces
1½ cups dried cranberries (or a 6-ounce package Craisins)
Grated peel (zest) of 2 lemons
1 egg
1 plus ⅛ cup buttermilk

Preheat the oven to 375°F. Lightly grease a baking sheet. In a food processor, blend the flour, sugar, salt, and baking powder. Add the cold butter, and pulse until the butter is about pea-size. Place the flour/butter mixture into a large bowl, and stir in the cranberries and lemon zest. In a small bowl, beat the egg, and combine it with 1 cup of the buttermilk. Add the egg/buttermilk mixture to the flour/cranberry mixture, stirring until just combined. On a floured surface, divide the dough into 2 equal parts. Pat the dough into two 8-inch rounds, each about ½-inch thick. Cut each round into 6 wedges. Place the wedges about 1 inch apart on the prepared baking sheet. Brush the tops with the remaining buttermilk (this will help the scones to lightly brown during baking). Bake for approximately 15 to 20 minutes, or until lightly browned. Remove the scones from baking sheet and serve warm.

Cherry-Orange Scones

Makes 16 small scones.

Scones:
2 cups all-purpose flour
2 tablespoons sugar
1 tablespoon baking powder
½ teaspoon salt
6 tablespoons chilled butter
1 tablespoon finely grated
    orange peel (zest)
¾ cup dried cherries
1 egg, lightly beaten
½ cup milk

Glaze:
1 cup powdered sugar
1 to 2 tablespoons orange juice
1 teaspoon finely grated orange
    peel (zest)

Preheat the oven to 400°F. Lightly grease a baking sheet. In a large bowl, combine the flour, sugar, baking powder, and salt. With a pastry blender, cut in the butter until the mixture resembles coarse crumbs. Stir in the grated orange peel and dried cherries. Make a well in the center of the dry mixture. In a small bowl, combine the egg and milk. Add the egg mixture all at once to the dry mixture. Using a fork, stir until the mixture clings together and forms a soft dough. Turn the dough out onto a lightly floured surface; knead gently about 15 times. Divide the dough into fourths; pat into squares about ½-inch thick. Cut each square diagonally twice to form 4 triangles. Place the triangles on the prepared baking sheet (or freeze at this point for future baking). Bake 15 minutes, or until lightly browned. To make the glaze, in a small bowl, combine powdered sugar, orange juice, and grated orange peel. Spoon the glaze over the hot scones; let cool for 5 minutes. Serve warm.

Carol's Corner
Rose and Jorge, our good friends next door, have been invaluable to me as "taste-testers." After sampling this recipe, Rose exclaimed, "These scones are out of this world!" And I agree.

(For inn information see page 40)

Date-Nut Coffee Cake Supreme

Makes about 10 servings.

Cake:
½ cup (1 stick) butter, room temperature
½ cup sugar
½ teaspoon vanilla extract
1 egg
1½ cups all-purpose flour
1½ teaspoons baking powder
½ teaspoon salt
½ cup milk

Filling:
¼ cup (½ stick) butter, melted
½ cup packed brown sugar
1 tablespoon all-purpose flour
1 tablespoon cinnamon
¼ cup chopped walnuts
¼ cup chopped dates

Topping:
¼ cup chopped walnuts

Preheat the oven to 350°F. Grease an 8-inch cake pan. In a medium bowl, beat together the butter, sugar, and vanilla. Beat in the egg. In another medium bowl, sift together the flour, baking powder, and salt. Add the sifted dry ingredients and the milk alternately to the egg mixture, beating after each addition. In a small bowl, combine the filling ingredients. Spread half the batter into the prepared pan. (The batter will be thick. To make spreading easier, drop the batter by small dollops, and then spread.) Sprinkle the filling evenly over the batter to within ½-inch of the pan edge. Spread the remaining batter over the filling. Top with the nuts. Bake for 35 to 45 minutes or until a wooden toothpick inserted near the center comes out clean. Cool on wire rack about 20 minutes. Serve warm or at room temperature.

(For inn information see page 18)

Mangels House

O riginally built in the 1880s, the Mangels House was the country home of Claus Mangels, who, together with his brother-in-law Claus Spreckels, founded the sugar beet industry in California. Situated on four acres of formal lawns, flower gardens, orchards, and woodlands, the Mangels House features large wraparound porches and borders the Forest of Nisene Marks and its ten thousand acres of redwoods, creeks, and trails. Off-site activities include golf, tennis, exploring the North Monterey Bay area, and attending local musical and theatrical events. Picturesque Monterey Bay is just a mile away.

Breakfast at this lovely Italianate Victorian includes seasonal fruits, scones and muffins, and an egg and cheese dish.

INNKEEPERS:	*Jacqueline & Ronald Fisher*
ADDRESS:	*570 Aptos Creek Road*
	Aptos, CA 95003
TELEPHONE:	*(831) 688-7982; (800) 320-7401*
E-MAIL:	*mangels@cruzio.com*
WEBSITE:	*www.innaccess.com/mangels*
ROOMS:	*6 Rooms; 1 Cottage; All with private baths*
CHILDREN:	*Children over the age of 11 are welcome*
ANIMALS:	*Prohibited; Resident dog and cats*

designated areas

Oatmeal Scones

Makes 12 scones.

2½ cups all-purpose flour
2 cups old-fashioned rolled oats
1 cup sugar
2 teaspoons baking powder
1 teaspoon baking soda
½ teaspoon salt
½ cup (1 stick) chilled butter, cut into small pieces
½ cup chilled shortening, cut into small pieces
Buttermilk (about ¾ cup)

In a food processor, combine the flour, oats, sugar, baking powder, baking soda, salt, butter, and shortening. Process until the mixture resembles coarse crumbs. When ready to make the scones, add just enough buttermilk to hold the dry ingredients together. Divide the dough in half. Pat each portion onto an ungreased cookie sheet into a circle about ¾-inch thick. Score each circle into 6 wedges, but do not separate. Preheat the oven to 375°F. Bake for 20 minutes, or until the scones are the desired color. Cut or break the scones apart. Serve warm.

Make-ahead tip: The dry, processed mixture can be kept in an airtight container in the refrigerator for an indefinite time.

Carol's Corner
Jacqueline at the Mangels House keeps the prepared dry, processed scone mixture on hand at all times. When she has guests, her formula is to use "one fistful per guest, plus one." She then adds just enough buttermilk to make the dough the proper consistency to pat onto the cookie sheet. Jacqueline says she receives many compliments on this easy recipe.

C. O. Packard House

Originally built in 1878, the C. O. Packard House bed and breakfast is one of four landmark homes on Executive Row in the historic village of Mendocino. This beautiful carpenter's Gothic Victorian is centrally located with easy access to local shops, beaches, trails, fine dining, and the Mendocino Headlands State Park. Formerly home to the town's chemist, the C. O. Packard House's four guest rooms each has a private bath with a jet-tub for two, glass-enclosed shower, luxury robes, slippers, television, and VCRs. Nearby are a plethora of activities to suit any taste, from bicycling, horseback riding, and scuba diving to museums, tours, and massages.

A bountiful breakfast is prepared in the French country kitchen and served in the elegant dining room.

INNKEEPERS:	*Maria & Dan Levin*
ADDRESS:	*45170 Little Lake Street*
	Mendocino, CA 95460
TELEPHONE:	*(707) 937-2677; (888) 453-2677*
E-MAIL:	*info@packardhouse.com*
WEBSITE:	*www.packardhouse.com*
ROOMS:	*4 Rooms; 1 Suite; All with private baths*
CHILDREN:	*Children over the age of 12 are welcome*
ANIMALS:	*Prohibited*

designated areas

Orange-Scented Scones

Makes 8 scones.

1¾ cups all-purpose flour
2 tablespoons baking powder
½ teaspoon kosher salt
1 tablespoon sugar
Grated peel (zest) of 1 medium orange
½ cup (1 stick) unsalted butter, chilled, cut into ⅓-inch cubes
⅔ cup plus 4 tablespoons buttermilk
2 tablespoons turbinado sugar (see Carol's Corner)

Preheat the oven to 400°F. Using the paddle attachment in an electric mixer, combine the flour, baking powder, salt, and sugar. Mix in the orange zest. Add the small butter cubes, and mix briefly until coated with flour mixture and no less than half their original size. With the mixer set on low speed, add the ⅔ cup buttermilk. Mix just until the buttermilk is absorbed and the dough begins to pull away from the sides of the bowl. With well-floured hands, shape the dough into a ball. On a lightly floured surface, pat the dough into a 7-inch circle. Cut the circle into fourths; then cut each fourth in half. Place the 8 triangular-shaped scones on a baking sheet lined with kitchen parchment paper. Brush the tops of the scones with the 4 tablespoons of buttermilk. Sprinkle with turbinado sugar. Bake the scones for 15 to 20 minutes until browned. Serve warm.

Carol's Corner
Turbinado sugar is a coarse granular sugar that is golden in color and has a mild molasses flavor. It can be found at most grocery stores, specialty food markets, and many coffee shops. One brand to look for is Sugar in the Raw.

Elk Cove Inn

Originally built in the 1870s by the L. E. White Lumber Company as an executive guest house, the two-story Elk Cove Inn eventually became one of the first bed and breakfasts on the northern California coast. Nestled in peaceful seclusion atop a bluff with nearly a mile of beachfront, this quiet retreat is totally surrounded by native trees, ocean, and rocks with some of the most spectacular views of the California coastline. The Victorian-style gazebo is perched on the edge of a bluff above the beach. During the spring and summer months, this favorite guest getaway is covered in Queen Anne's lace and other wildflowers.

Shops and restaurants are within easy walking distance. The historic village of Mendocino is just twenty minutes north, and the fabulous Anderson Valley wineries and redwood forests are a short drive away.

All guest rooms have feather beds, down comforters, vintage linens, rocking chairs, window seats or sofas, and fresh flowers. Flashlights are provided for nighttime beach excursions.

A typical breakfast begins with a delicious baked pear filled with almond and fruit-flavored cream cheese followed by mouth-watering entrées.

INNKEEPER:	*Elaine Bryant*
ADDRESS:	*6300 Hwy 1 South*
	Elk, CA 95432
TELEPHONE:	*(707) 877-3321; (800) 275-2967*
E-MAIL:	*innkeeper@elkcoveinn.com*
WEBSITE:	*www.elkcoveinn.com*
ROOMS:	*6 Rooms; 4 Suites; 4 Cottages; Private baths*
CHILDREN:	*Children over the age of 12 are welcome*
ANIMALS:	*Prohibited; Resident dog and cat*

call first

Orange Scones

Makes 12 scones.

Scones:
1¾ cups all-purpose flour
1½ teaspoons baking powder
½ teaspoon baking soda
⅓ cup sugar
Grated peel (zest) of 1 orange
½ cup (1 stick) butter, room temperature
½ cup orange juice
1 egg, beaten

Glaze:
½ cup powdered sugar
1 tablespoon orange juice

Preheat the oven to 375°F. Grease a cookie sheet. In a medium bowl, sift together the flour, baking powder, baking soda, and sugar. Mix in the orange zest. Using a pastry blender, cut in the butter until the mixture resembles coarse crumbs. Make a well in the center of the dry ingredients. In a small bowl, combine the orange juice and egg. Add all at once to the dry ingredients. Using a fork, stir just until moistened. Drop 12 equal mounds of dough onto the prepared cookie sheet. Bake for 12 to 15 minutes, or until golden brown. Cool on a wire rack.

To prepare the glaze, in a small bowl, combine the powdered sugar and orange juice. Mix until smooth. Spread a small amount of the glaze on each scone and serve.

The General's Daughter Scones

Makes 12 to 18 scones.

3 cups all-purpose flour
1½ tablespoons baking powder
1 teaspoon salt
2 plus 2 tablespoons sugar
7 ounces dried fruit (any type)
15 ounces plus 4 tablespoons heavy cream

Preheat the oven to 350°F. Combine the flour, baking powder, salt, 2 tablespoons of sugar, and dried fruit in an electric mixer using a dough hook. With the mixer on low, add 15 ounces of cream until the mixture comes together as dough. Roll out the dough ½ inch thick, cut into triangles, and place on a cookie sheet lined with parchment paper or greased with oil. Brush lightly with the remaining cream and sprinkle with the remaining sugar. Bake for approximately 20 minutes or until golden brown.

(For inn information see page 44)

Union Street Inn Scones

Makes 12 scones.

Instead of using the traditional method of rolling out the dough and cutting it into triangle shapes, this timesaving scone recipe skips those steps, and the dough is spooned directly onto the baking sheet.

2½ cups baking mix (such as Bisquick)
3 tablespoons sugar
4 tablespoons (½ stick) chilled butter, grated
¼ cup dried cranberries
¼ cup raisins
Grated peel (zest) from 1 orange
1 apple or fresh pear, peeled, cored, and grated
½ cup milk

Preheat the oven to 425°F. Grease a baking sheet. In a large bowl, combine the baking mix, sugar, butter, cranberries, raisins, orange, and apple or pear. Slowly add the milk to the rest of the ingredients, a small amount at a time, and stir with a fork. Keep stirring and adding milk in small amounts until the dough just holds together. (The dough should not be too wet—you may have some milk left over.) Drop the dough by spoonfuls (in 12 equal portions) one inch apart onto the prepared baking sheet. Bake for approximately 12 minutes, or until the scones are lightly browned. Remove scones from the baking sheet, and serve warm.

(For inn information see page 22)

Aptos Beach Inn

O riginally built in 1867 as a replica of Abraham Lincoln's Springfield home, the Aptos Beach Inn offers activities and amenities of a modern ocean-side resort. All rooms include a queen- or king-size bed, private bath, fireplace, and bathrobes. The inn also provides a number of activities, including volleyball, tennis, croquet, badminton, swimming, bird-watching, or curling up with a good book from the library. Whether playing tennis or walking on the beach, guests find the inn a place to revitalize and relax.

Nestled between spectacular beaches and lush green fields, the inn was the first house built in the Pajaro Valley and was visited and photographed by Ansel Adams.

INNKEEPERS: *Susan Van Horn & Brian Denny*
ADDRESS: *1258 San Andreas Road*
La Selva Beach, CA 95076
TELEPHONE: *(831) 728-1000; (888) 523-2244*
E-MAIL: *innkeeper@aptosbeachinn.com*
WEBSITE: *www.aptosbeachinn.com*
ROOMS: *4 Rooms; 1 Suite; All with private baths*
CHILDREN: *Welcome*
ANIMALS: *Prohibited*

designated areas

Yogurt Coffee Cake

Makes 12 servings.

<u>Streusel topping:</u>
⅔ cup all-purpose flour
⅔ cup light brown sugar
1 teaspoon cinnamon
¼ teaspoon salt
⅔ cup chopped pecans
5 tablespoons unsalted butter, chilled, cut into small pieces

<u>Batter:</u>
2 cups all-purpose flour
1 teaspoon baking powder
½ teaspoon salt
1¼ cups plain yogurt
1 teaspoon vanilla extract
1 cup sugar
4 tablespoons butter, room temperature
2 large eggs

To make the streusel topping, in a medium bowl, combine the ⅔ cup of the flour, brown sugar, cinnamon, salt, pecans, and the chilled butter with a fork or pastry blender until the mixture resembles coarse crumbs.

To make the batter, in another medium bowl, sift together the 2 cups flour, baking powder, and salt. In a small bowl, stir together the yogurt and vanilla extract. In a large bowl, using a fork, combine the sugar and room-temperature butter. Beat in the eggs one at a time. With a whisk, beat in the flour mixture in three parts alternately with the yogurt mixture. Preheat the oven to 350°F. Spread the batter evenly in a greased 13x9-inch pan. Sprinkle with the streusel topping. Bake for 25 to 30 minutes. Cool briefly on a wire rack. Serve warm.

Make-ahead tip: Streusel Topping may be made a day or more in advance. Refrigerate until ready to use.

Baked Apple Pancake
Baked Pear Pancakes
Lemon Poppy Seed Pancakes
Lemon Soufflé Pancakes
Oatmeal-Buttermilk Pancakes
Orange Pancakes with Orange Syrup
Perfect Lemon Pancakes
Puffed Oven-Baked Pancake
Pumpkin Whole-Wheat Pancakes
Blintz Soufflé
Ricotta Pancakes

Pancakes, Waffles, & Blintz Soufflé

Quail Mountain

Located on twenty-six acres and three hundred feet above Napa Valley, the Quail Mountain bed and breakfast is surrounded by redwood, madrona, manzanita, oak, and Douglas fir trees. Each of the three guest rooms boasts a king-size bed, private bathroom, and individual deck. The comfortable beds have goose down comforters and pillows with handmade quilt covers.

Local activities include hiking, bicycling, balloon rides, golfing, climbing, soaking in mud baths, and visiting local wineries. Three wineries are within walking distance.

A tasty breakfast is served in the solarium or on one of the many decks. Whether it's delightful French toast or delectable waffles, all recipes are specially selected and accompanied by Quail Mountain's very own blend of Thanksgiving Coffee.

INNKEEPER:	*Eric Amadei*
ADDRESS:	*4455 North Saint Helena Hwy*
	Calistoga, CA 94515
TELEPHONE:	*(707) 942-0316*
E-MAIL:	*www.quailmtn.com*
WEBSITE:	*www.quailmtn.com*
ROOMS:	*2 Rooms; 1 Suite; All with private baths*
CHILDREN:	*Unsuitable*
ANIMALS:	*Prohibited*

Baked Apple Pancake

Makes 6 servings.

3 large or 4 medium Granny
  Smith or Golden Delicious
  apples
4 tablespoons lemon juice
5 tablespoons powdered sugar
1½ teaspoons cinnamon
½ plus ¼ cup butter
6 large eggs
1 cup milk
1 cup flour
1 teaspoon salt
¼ teaspoon baking powder

Garnish suggestions:
Cranberry relish
Cherry preserves
Tart cherries
Fresh berries
Chopped nuts
Powdered sugar
Whipped cream
Syrup

Peel, core, and cut the apples into ¼-inch slices; place the slices in a large bowl. Add the lemon juice and stir. In a small bowl, mix the powdered sugar and cinnamon together. Add to the apples and lemon juice. Mix thoroughly. In a 12- or 13-inch ovenproof skillet with sloping sides, melt the ½ cup butter. Add the apple mixture, and cook on medium heat for 10 to 12 minutes. Move the rack in the oven to the center position. Preheat the oven to 425°F. In a small saucepan or microwave, melt the remaining ¼ cup butter and cool slightly. In a large bowl, beat together the eggs and milk. In another bowl, sift together the flour, salt, and baking powder. Add the flour mixture to the egg mixture in 3 or 4 stages, mixing after each addition. Add the melted butter and mix again. Pour the batter over the cooked apples in the skillet. Place the skillet in the hot oven, and bake for approximately 27 minutes. Remove from the oven, and with a heat-resistant rubber spatula, loosen the pancake from the sides and bottom of the skillet. Wearing oven mitts, place a large serving plate over the skillet and invert to remove the pancake. To serve, decorate the pancake with one or more of the garnish suggestions.

Old Monterey Inn

Surrounded by over an acre of English gardens, the Old Monterey Inn is a 1929 Tudor-style manor house that offers an enchanting hideaway in the heart of Monterey. This historic inn is the perfect getaway for travelers bound for Monterey Peninsula, Carmel, Pebble Beach or Big Sur. The grounds provide lovely views from each of the elegantly appointed rooms. Each room has a private bath and sitting area. Many have authentic wood-burning fireplaces, stained glass windows and skylights.

Guests can actually hear the sounds of the waves and the barking of the sea lions from nearby Monterey Bay. Points of interest include Monterey Bay Aquarium, Cannery Row, Fisherman's Wharf, Point Lobos State Reserve, and the lone cypress.

A gourmet breakfast, afternoon refreshments, and evening hors d'oeuvres with complimentary beverages are served daily.

INNKEEPERS:	*Ann & Gene Swett*
ADDRESS:	*500 Martin Street*
	Monterey, CA 93940
TELEPHONE:	*(831) 375-8284; (800) 350-2344*
E-MAIL:	*omi@oldmontereyinn.com*
WEBSITE:	*www.oldmontereyinn.com*
ROOMS:	*8 Rooms; 2 Suites; All with private baths*
CHILDREN:	*Children over the age of 12 are welcome*
ANIMALS:	*Prohibited*

Baked Pear Pancakes

Makes 6 servings.

Bartlett, Anjou, and Bosc pears are excellent varieties to use when baking. Want to make an impression? These Baked Pear Pancakes present beautifully when topped with colorful fresh berries.

6 eggs
1 cup whole milk
1 cup all-purpose flour
4 tablespoons melted butter
½ teaspoon almond extract
2 teaspoons grated lemon
   peel (zest)
3 large baking pears, ripe but
   firm

2 tablespoons powdered sugar
3 tablespoons lemon juice
Powdered sugar, for garnish
Fresh berries (or other seasonal
   fresh fruit), for garnish
Syrup, for serving

Coat 6 shallow, individual baking dishes (5- or 6-inch diameter) with nonstick cooking spray. In a blender or bowl, mix the eggs and milk. Blend in the flour. While stirring, drizzle the melted butter into the egg mixture. Add the almond extract and lemon zest. Preheat the oven to 425°F. Peel the pears, cut each in half, and core. Cut each half into 5 or 6 slices. In a medium bowl, combine the powdered sugar and lemon juice. Gently toss the pear slices in the juice mixture; drain. Lay 5 or 6 pear slices on the bottom of each dish. Pour ½ cup of the batter over the pears. Bake for 20 minutes. To serve, sprinkle each pancake with the powdered sugar, decorate with the berries, and pass the syrup.

Note: These pancakes can be made without layering the fruit before baking. The pancakes will still puff up around the edges and make a "bowl," which can be filled with whatever fruit is in season.

Make-ahead tip: This batter mixture may be made the day before and refrigerated 8 to 10 hours. When ready to cook, let the batter come to room temperature before using.

Thistle Dew Inn

T he two homes that comprise the Thistle Dew Inn were originally built in 1869 and 1910. Both have ceilings over eleven feet high, and the common rooms reflect the graciousness and scale of the period. The inn is furnished with an impressive collection of museum-quality arts and crafts furniture, hand-made quilts, and unusual antiques. Mimosa, the largest of six guest rooms, features a cozy fireplace, a luxurious two-person whirlpool tub in an Italian terra cotta-tiled bath, and a private deck with an antique porch swing.

The innkeepers of the Thistle Dew Inn offer bicycles, helmets, locks, daypacks, and even picnic baskets free-of-charge to their guests. A nearby bike path leads to a myriad of local wineries, vineyards, and historical points of interest.

Sumptuous breakfast delights include raisin bread French toast with real maple syrup, ham and fruit, oven baked "Dutch babies" topped with homemade preserves, and lemon poppy seed pancakes with honey butter.

INNKEEPERS: *Larry & Norma Barnett*
ADDRESS: *171 West Spain Street*
Sonoma, CA 95476
TELEPHONE: *(707) 938-2909; (800) 382-7895*
E-MAIL: *tdibandb@aol.com*
WEBSITE: *www.thistledew.com*
ROOMS: *4 Rooms; 2 Suites; All with private baths*
CHILDREN: *Children under the age of 12 are discouraged*
ANIMALS: *Prohibited*

designated areas

Lemon Poppy Seed Pancakes

Makes 30 pancakes (4 inches diameter).

Thistle Dew Inn serves these lemon-flavored pancakes topped with Honey Butter (recipe on page 144). A very good flavor combination.

3 cups unbleached white flour
2 tablespoons baking powder
1 teaspoon baking soda
½ teaspoon salt
4 tablespoons poppy seeds
1 cup quick-cooking oatmeal (not instant)
Grated lemon peel (zest) of 2 lemons
5 eggs
1 cup sour cream
1½ cups milk
1½ cups water
1 teaspoon lemon oil (for cooking—not furniture polish)
½ teaspoon vanilla extract or vanilla powder
Honey Butter (recipe on page 144)
Maple syrup, optional

In a large bowl, sift together the flour, baking powder, baking soda, and salt. Stir in the poppy seeds, oatmeal and lemon zest. In a separate bowl, beat together the eggs, sour cream, milk, water, lemon oil, and vanilla extract. Add this mixture to the flour/poppy seed mixture, and stir until combined. Let the batter stand for 30 minutes. (The batter will thicken. If necessary, add a little more water to make the batter the right consistency.) Heat a griddle until moderately hot; butter the griddle. Drop the batter by ¼ cupfuls onto the griddle, leaving at least a 1-inch space between the pancakes. When bubbles form on the tops of the pancakes and the undersides are golden brown, turn the pancakes over, and cook second sides until done. Serve with Honey Butter and, if desired, maple syrup.

Sea Rock

S urrounded by century-old cypress trees, beautifully landscaped gardens, and spacious lawns, the Sea Rock bed and breakfast inn offers spectacular panoramic views of the Pacific Ocean and the rocky cliffs of Mendocino Headlands State Park. All deluxe units include private entrances and decks, woodburning fireplaces, king-size beds and telephones with computer jacks.

Breakfast is a delight at the Sea Rock. An expanded continental breakfast buffet is served each morning in the breakfast room that overlooks the ocean. Fresh fruit, juices, muffins, yogurt, and excellent coffees and herb teas are all included in the buffet. From the breakfast room, guests might observe playful seals, migrating whales, and soaring sea birds.

INNKEEPERS:	*Susie & Andy Plocher*
ADDRESS:	*11101 Lansing Street*
	Mendocino, CA 95460
TELEPHONE:	*(707) 937-0926; (800) 906-0926*
E-MAIL:	*aplocher@mcn.org*
WEBSITE:	*www.searock.com*
ROOMS:	*8 Suites; 6 Cottages; Private baths*
CHILDREN:	*Unsuitable*
ANIMALS:	*Prohibited*

Lemon Soufflé Pancakes

Makes 20 to 24 pancakes (3 inches in diameter).

The name is very fitting—these lemon-flavored pancakes have a light, airy soufflé-like texture. They present beautifully with a spoonful of fresh red raspberries, a dollop of whipped cream, and topped with a sprinkling of lemon zest.

6 eggs
⅔ cup all-purpose flour
1½ cups ricotta cheese
½ cup (1 stick) butter, melted and cooled slightly
4 tablespoons sugar
½ teaspoon salt
4 tablespoons grated lemon peel (zest)

Optional accompaniments:
Raspberry syrup (recipe on page 147)
Maple syrup
Fresh red raspberries
Whipped cream
Additional grated lemon peel (zest)

Separate the eggs, putting the whites in a medium bowl and the yolks in a large bowl. Beat the whites until they hold peaks. In the large bowl, combine the egg yolks with the flour, ricotta cheese, melted butter, sugar, salt, and lemon zest until well mixed. With a large spoon or a rubber spatula, gently fold the whites into the yolk mixture. There should still be small pieces of egg white showing. For each pancake, drop the batter by ¼ cupfuls onto a lightly greased griddle (or skillet) on medium heat. Cook slowly for about 1½ minutes. Turn the pancakes; cook the second side about 1 minute or until done. The pancakes can be kept in a 250°F. oven (up to 30 minutes) until ready to serve. Garnish the pancakes with the fresh raspberries, whipped cream, and grated lemon zest. Offer the raspberry or maple syrup on the side.

Grieb Farmhouse Inn

S ituated among the walnut and oak groves of California's central coast, the Grieb Farmhouse Inn was originally built in 1888 by Konrad Grieb and was surrounded by acres of walnut, apricot, and oak trees. Years later, the house was sold to a family with sixteen children. In 1975, a new owner removed one wing and totally renovated the house. Twenty-two years later, the farmhouse, now in the middle of a residential neighborhood, was refurbished by the current owners and opened as a bed and breakfast inn.

Staying at the Grieb Farmhouse Inn is like visiting with an old friend. Shortly after arriving, guests are treated to late afternoon snacks and beverages. Each morning, a savory gourmet breakfast, which includes a fruit-dish appetizer, baked breads, muffins and scones, gingerbread pancakes, strawberry crepes, omelets, sourdough pancakes, and stuffed French toast is served in the dining room or outside in the garden.

The inn was awarded the Arroyo Grande Chamber of Commerce Beautification Award.

INNKEEPERS:	*Pam & Mike Clare*
ADDRESS:	*851 Todd Lane*
	Arroyo Grande, CA 93420
TELEPHONE:	*(805) 481-8540*
E-MAIL:	*info@griebfarmhouseinn.com*
WEBSITE:	*www.griebfarmhouseinn.com*
ROOMS:	*2 Rooms; Both with private baths*
CHILDREN:	*Unsuitable*
ANIMALS:	*Prohibited*

designated areas

Oatmeal-Buttermilk Pancakes

Makes 16 pancakes (4½ inches in diameter).

Make the batter for these Swedish pancakes the day before, or at least two hours ahead, since the mixture needs to "rest" before cooking.

2 cups oatmeal, old-fashioned or quick-cooking (not instant)
½ cup all-purpose flour
3 tablespoons sugar
1 teaspoon baking soda
1 teaspoon baking powder
½ teaspoon salt
2½ cups buttermilk
2 eggs
4 tablespoons (½ stick) butter, melted
1 teaspoon vanilla extract
Syrup, for serving

In a large bowl, combine the oatmeal, flour, sugar, baking soda, baking powder, and salt. Make a well in the center of the dry mixture. In a medium bowl, combine the buttermilk, eggs, melted butter, and vanilla. Add the wet ingredients all at once to the dry mixture; stir just until moistened. Cover the bowl and refrigerate. Let the batter stand for at least two hours to thicken. To make the pancakes, drop the batter by ¼ cupfuls onto a hot, lightly greased griddle or heavy skillet. Cook over medium heat about two minutes, or until the tops of the pancakes are bubbly and edges are slightly dry. Turn the pancakes; cook the second side until golden. Serve with your favorite syrup.

Inn at Occidental

Nestled in the heart of Sonoma County, the Inn at Occidental embodies the spirit of the valley where vineyards, redwoods, and coastal scenery provide an unparalleled beauty. Completely restored and furnished with antiques, family heirlooms, and original artwork, the inn is an ideal location for meetings and glorious wine country weddings. Guests relax in the common rooms or in the English cottage garden with its moss-mantled fountain.

Breakfast includes fresh fruit, juices, granola, luscious baked pastries, and delicious hot entrées. The private herb garden provides wonderful flavorings that enhance the entrées that feature the best of Sonoma County's produce. Served fireside or, weather permitting, on the outdoor patio or at one of the umbrella-covered tables, guests leave feeling satisfied. Complimentary Sonoma County wine and appetizing hors d'oeuvres are served in the early evening.

INNKEEPERS: *Jack, Bill, and Jean Ballard*
ADDRESS: *3657 Church Street*
Occidental, CA 95465
TELEPHONE: *(707) 874-1047; (800) 522-6324*
E-MAIL: *innkeeper@innatoccidental.com*
WEBSITE: *www.innatoccidental.com*
ROOMS: *14 Rooms; 2 Suites; 1 Cottage; Private baths*
CHILDREN: *Children over the age of 12 welcome; Children under the age of 12 welcome in cottage only*
ANIMALS: *Welcome in cottage; Resident cat*

designated areas

Orange Pancakes
with Orange Syrup

Makes 12 pancakes (5 inches in diameter).

A delightful double dose of orange flavor, these terrific pancakes are topped with warm Orange Syrup (recipe on page 146).

2 cups flour
2 teaspoons baking soda
1 teaspoon salt
¼ cup sugar

2 eggs
1¾ cups orange juice
¼ cup (½ stick) butter, melted

In a large bowl, sift together the flour, baking soda, salt, and sugar. In a medium bowl, beat together the eggs, orange juice, and melted butter. Add the wet ingredients to the dry ingredients. Stir with a spoon to combine; the batter will be slightly lumpy. Grease a griddle (or skillet) with vegetable oil. Heat until moderately hot. Using a ⅓-cup measure, pour the batter onto the griddle, leaving a 1-inch space between the pancakes. When bubbles form on the top of the pancakes, and the undersides are light brown, turn the pancakes over, and cook until the other sides are brown. Serve with the warm Orange Syrup (recipe on page 146).

Gerstle Park Inn

The Gerstle Park Inn is a landmark estate that for over one hundred years has graced the heritage oak-laden foothills of Marin. An extensive renovation has produced an elegant, fully appointed inn. The handsome Douglas Fir wood-paneled conference room is available for meetings of twenty people or fewer. Guests enjoy luxurious accommodations, including fine linens, sumptuous bathrobes, excellent mattresses, down comforters, and complimentary evening wine and snacks.

Within a leisurely walk from the inn's lovely verandah are inviting neighborhood restaurants and shops. San Francisco, Berkeley, and wine country are just thirty minutes away. Local activities include golf, horseback riding, balloon rides, tall ship sailing, boat rentals, kayaking, fishing, hang gliding, and hiking.

INNKEEPERS: *Jim & Judy Dowling*
ADDRESS: *34 Grove Street*
San Rafael, CA 94901
TELEPHONE: *(415) 721-7611; (800) 726-7611*
E-MAIL: *innkeeper@gerstleparkinn.com*
WEBSITE: *www.gerstleparkinn.com*
ROOMS: *8 Junior Suites; 2 Carriage House Units; All with private baths*
CHILDREN: *Unsuitable*
ANIMALS: *Prohibited*

designated areas

Perfect Lemon Pancakes

Makes 6 servings (3 pancakes each).

The name says it all. These pancakes are perfection.

6 large eggs, whites and yolks separated
½ cup unbleached flour
1½ cups low-fat cottage cheese, small curd
½ cup (1 stick) unsalted butter, melted and cooled slightly
4 tablespoons sugar
½ teaspoon salt
2 tablespoons grated lemon peel (zest)
Powdered sugar, for garnish
Maple syrup
Fresh fruit (strawberries and blueberries are especially good with
  these pancakes)

In a large bowl, combine the egg yolks, flour, cottage cheese, melted butter, sugar, salt, and lemon zest. In a separate bowl, beat the egg whites until soft peaks form. Carefully fold the beaten whites into the batter mixture until just blended. Heat a large nonstick griddle over medium heat until hot. Coat with nonstick cooking spray. Using a ¼-cup measure, pour the batter onto the griddle, leaving a 1-inch space between the pancakes. Adjust the heat to medium low. Cook until the under sides of the pancakes are lightly browned. Turn pancakes over and cook the other side until done. To serve, place 3 pancakes on each plate. Sprinkle with the powdered sugar and accompany with the syrup and fresh fruit.

Carol's Corner
During a McCollum family reunion in Estes Park, Colorado, my nephew Todd came up with a super idea when he tasted these wonderful lemon pancakes. He suggested using the same batter for making lemon dessert crêpes. We tried it, and it worked perfectly! Just spread the batter on the griddle thinly and evenly. Cook briefly on each side. Fill the crêpes with fruit, roll them up, dust them with powdered sugar, and top with whipped cream. Delicious!

Hope-Bosworth House & Hope-Merrill House

Located in the captivating town of Geyserville, the charming Queen Anne Hope-Bosworth House and the striking Victorian Hope-Merrill House offer rooms that are a step into the past. Polished fir floors and antique light fixtures enhance the period furnishings.

Both inns offer a grand view of Geyser Peak, the world's largest geothermal field.

INNKEEPERS:	*Cosette & Ron Scheiber*
ADDRESS:	*21253 Geyserville Avenue*
	Geyserville, CA 95441
TELEPHONE:	*(707) 857-3356; (800) 825-4233*
E-MAIL:	*moreinfo@hope-inns.com*
WEBSITE:	*www.hope-inns.com*
ROOMS:	*12 Rooms; All with private baths*
CHILDREN:	*Unsuitable*
ANIMALS:	*Prohibited*

designated areas

Puffed Oven-Baked Pancake

Makes 1 serving.

This recipe, also known as "Dutch Babies," makes enough batter for one individual pancake. For larger groups, increase the recipe, and bake the pancakes in several individual skillets or small baking dishes. To make one large pancake for serving a group, see variation below.

2 tablespoons unsalted butter
1 egg
¼ cup low-fat milk
¼ cup unbleached all-purpose flour
¼ teaspoon almond extract, optional
¼ teaspoon lemon zest, optional

Topping suggestions:
Powdered sugar
Sliced strawberries or other fresh fruit
Oven-toasted pecans
Syrup

Preheat the oven to 475°F. Place the butter in a 4-inch ovenproof skillet or other similar-size baking dish. Place the skillet in the oven to melt the butter. (Watch carefully so it doesn't burn; it doesn't take long.) In a small bowl, beat the egg well. Gradually beat in the milk, then the flour, and mix until smooth. Stir in the almond extract and lemon zest. Pour the batter into the hot skillet containing the melted butter, and return the skillet to the oven. Bake until the pancake is puffed and golden, about 12 minutes. Serve at once, accompanied by one or more toppings of choice.

Variation: To make one large pancake, multiply all the ingredients by the number of people you wish to serve, and increase the pan size accordingly. When making a larger pancake, one idea is to spread the cooked pancake with selected toppings, roll up jelly-roll fashion, and cut crosswise into slices.

La Chaumiere

Located on a picturesque residential street in Calistoga, La Chaumiere offers an abundance of beautiful flowers. The brick courtyard boasts an intimate grouping of cascading plants. Guests relax to the melodic sounds of water fountains while reading a book or watching the hummingbirds at the feeder. A stairway leads to a second story tree house that surrounds a large redwood tree. During the summer months, a local masseuse does massages for guests in the tree house. The landscaping has been kept simple to accentuate the rustic feel of the rough whole-timber redwood uprights and crossbeams. The cottage décor is a blend of country cottage and Southwestern styles. Conveniently located on a picturesque residential street, this unique inn is only a short walk from the delightful downtown Calistoga shops, restaurants, and spas.

The innkeeper offers concierge service to his guests.

INNKEEPER:	*Gary Venturi*
ADDRESS:	*1301 Cedar Street*
	Calistoga, CA 94515
TELEPHONE:	*(707) 942-5139; (800) 474-6800*
E-MAIL:	*calist9578@aol.com*
WEBSITE:	*www.lachaumiere.com*
ROOMS:	*2 Rooms; 1 Cottage; All with private baths*
CHILDREN:	*Children over the age of 12 are welcome*
ANIMALS:	*Prohibited*

designated areas

Pumpkin Whole-Wheat Pancakes

Makes 16 pancakes (4½ inches in diameter).

1 cup whole-wheat flour
1 cup all-purpose flour
½ teaspoon salt
2 tablespoons baking powder
1 teaspoon cinnamon
½ teaspoon nutmeg
2 tablespoons brown sugar
2 eggs
½ cup canned pumpkin
2 cups milk
¼ cup vegetable oil
Syrup, for serving

In a large bowl, combine the whole-wheat flour, all-purpose flour, salt, baking powder, cinnamon, nutmeg, and brown sugar. Make a well in the center of the dry mixture. In a small bowl, slightly beat the eggs, and combine them with the pumpkin, milk, and oil. Pour the wet mixture into the well in the dry ingredients. Stir gently just until the dry ingredients are moistened. Let the batter stand for 5 minutes. After it stands, if the batter seems too thick, a small amount of milk may be added to obtain the desired consistency. To make the pancakes, drop the batter by ¼ cupfuls for each pancake onto a hot, lightly greased griddle or heavy skillet. Cook over medium heat about 2 minutes, or until the tops of the pancakes are bubbly and edges are slightly dry. Turn the pancakes; cook the other side until golden brown. Serve with your favorite syrup.

Blintz Soufflé

Makes 4 large or 6 small servings.

A great twist on the usual time-consuming blintzes. This breakfast dish must be started the night before, but it couldn't be any easier because you start with ready-made frozen blintzes. It takes only minutes to prepare, and in the morning you just pop it into the oven. A colorful fruit cup and bacon or sausage will round out this delicious meal.

¼ cup (½ stick) butter or margarine
6 to 8 frozen cheese blintzes (or blueberry or cherry)
5 eggs, beaten
1¼ cups sour cream
⅓ cup orange juice
⅔ cup sugar (or slightly less, if desired)
1 tablespoon vanilla extract

In an 11x7-inch glass baking dish, melt the butter in the microwave on low power so the butter doesn't splatter. (Or melt the butter in a saucepan, and pour it into the baking dish.) Lay the frozen blintzes on top of the melted butter in a single layer. In a medium bowl, mix together the beaten eggs, sour cream, orange juice, sugar, and vanilla. Pour the mixture over the blintzes. Cover and refrigerate 8 to 10 hours. When ready to cook, preheat the oven to 350°F. Bake for approximately 50 minutes, or until the blintz soufflé is set. Cut into portions, serving one or two blintzes per person.

(For inn information see page 18)

Ricotta Pancakes

Makes about 10 to 12 pancakes.

3 eggs, separated
⅔ cup milk
1 cup ricotta cheese
½ cup flour
1 teaspoon baking powder
½ teaspoon salt

In a medium bowl, beat together the egg yolks, milk, ricotta cheese, flour, baking powder, and salt. In a small bowl, beat the egg whites until stiff. Gently fold the beaten egg whites into the egg yolk/flour mixture. Heat a greased griddle until moderately hot. Using a ¼-cup measure, drop the batter onto a hot griddle, leaving a 1-inch space between the pancakes. When the pancakes are puffed and lightly browned on the bottom, turn the pancakes over and cook until the other sides are done.

Serving suggestions: Serve the pancakes with lemon sauce or a berry sauce with a dollop of sour cream or whipped cream. Or serve them with a dollop of apricot or strawberry jam and sour cream. Garnish with fresh berries and kiwi slices.

(For inn information see page 98)

Baked French Toast

Blueberry French Toast

Breakfast Granola

Caramel Apple French Toast

Croissant French Toast

Croissant French Toast à l'Orange

Custard Baked French Toast

Decadent French Toast Soufflé

*Fluffy Vanilla & Cinnamon French Toast
   with Bananas & Almonds*

Homemade Granola

Judy's French Toast with Fruit Syrup

Overnight Praline French Toast

Panettone French Toast

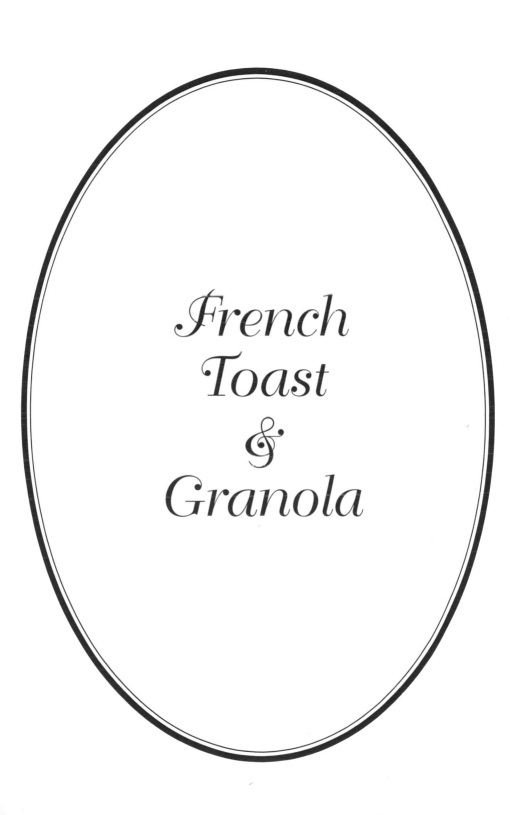

French
Toast
&
Granola

Baked French Toast

Makes 6 to 8 servings.

This is one of those wonderful, coveted, make-ahead breakfast recipes. By assembling this French toast the night before, most of the work is done, and you get to stay in bed longer in the morning. If you choose to make the Cabernet wine jelly syrup with the dried fruit mentioned in the variation below, it, too, must be started the night before serving.

1 (16-ounce) loaf French bread, cut into cubes
1 (8-ounce) package cream cheese, cut into small pieces
10 eggs
1½ cups half-and-half
¼ cup maple syrup
½ cup (1 stick) melted butter, slightly cooled
Powdered sugar for garnish
Additional maple syrup for topping (or use syrup variation below)
Cabernet wine jelly and dried fruit (if syrup variation is used)

Coat a 13x9-inch baking dish with nonstick cooking spray. Layer half of the bread cubes in the prepared dish. Scatter the cream cheese pieces evenly over the bread cubes. Cover with the remaining bread cubes. In a large bowl, beat together the eggs, half-and-half, maple syrup, and melted butter. Pour the egg mixture over the bread cubes. Press the bread down to absorb the egg mixture. Cover and refrigerate overnight. In the morning, preheat the oven to 350°F. Bake for 40 to 50 minutes, or until the French toast is puffed and lightly browned. Cut into serving pieces, dust with the powdered sugar, and offer the syrup on the side.

Variation: Instead of maple syrup, try the French toast with melted Cabernet wine jelly. Heat the jelly slightly to syrup consistency. If desired, soak the dried fruit in the melted jelly overnight. Reheat the jelly/dried fruit mixture before serving over the French toast.

(For inn information see page 62)

Blueberry French Toast

Makes 6 servings.

French toast:
1 baguette (a 24-inch loaf of
  French bread)
6 large eggs
3 cups milk
½ teaspoon ground nutmeg
¼ teaspoon salt
1 teaspoon vanilla extract
¾ plus ¼ cup brown sugar

1 cup pecan halves
4 tablespoons plus 1 teaspoon
  butter
2 cups blueberries (12 ounces)

Blueberry syrup:
1 cup blueberries
½ cup maple syrup
1 tablespoon lemon juice

To make the French toast, grease a 13x9-inch baking dish. Cut 20 (1-inch thick) slices from the baguette. Arrange the slices in the baking dish, trimming crusts, if necessary, to fit. In a large bowl, whisk together the eggs, milk, nutmeg, salt, vanilla, and the ¾ cup brown sugar. Pour or ladle the mixture over the bread slices. Cover and refrigerate overnight. In the morning, preheat the oven to 350°F. In a shallow pan, spread the pecans evenly. Toast in the oven until fragrant, about 8 minutes. Toss the pecans with the 1 teaspoon butter. Increase the oven to 400°F. Remove the bread mixture from refrigerator, and sprinkle the pecans and blueberries over the top. In a saucepan over low heat, melt the remaining 4 tablespoons butter, and add the remaining ¼ cup brown sugar, stirring until melted and well combined. Drizzle the butter mixture over the pecans and blueberries. Bake for 20 to 30 minutes until set and liquid from blueberries is bubbling. Serve with warm blueberry syrup.

To make the syrup, in a small saucepan, cook the blueberries and maple syrup over medium heat until the berries burst, about 3 minutes. Pour the syrup through a sieve, pressing solids, and stir in the lemon juice.

Make-ahead tip: Syrup may be made a day ahead. Cover and refrigerate. Reheat before serving.

(For inn information see page 70)

Breakfast Granola

Makes about 10 cups granola.

This recipe, a favorite of guests at Ramekins bed and breakfast, may be doubled or tripled to feed a crowd. How about baking a batch for your next family reunion? Because granola freezes well, you can easily make it in advance. Warning: Stand by for oodles of compliments.

5 cups old-fashioned rolled oats
1 cup cashews
1 cup sliced almonds
½ cup packed light brown sugar
1 tablespoon grated orange peel (zest)
½ tablespoon cinnamon
½ teaspoon grated nutmeg
1 cup (2 sticks) butter
⅓ cup maple syrup
½ cup golden raisins
½ cup dried cherries or dried cranberries
½ cup chopped dates

Preheat the oven to 325°F. Line a 17x11-inch rimmed baking sheet with kitchen parchment paper. In a very large stainless steel bowl, combine the rolled oats, cashews, almonds, brown sugar, orange zest, cinnamon, and nutmeg. In a saucepan, heat the butter and syrup together, stirring until the butter is melted and well combined with the syrup. Thoroughly mix the butter/syrup mixture with the dry mixture. Spread evenly over the prepared baking sheet. Bake for approximately 40 minutes (stir once or twice during baking) until golden brown and stuck together. Allow the granola to cool on the baking sheet before breaking it into pieces. Add the dried fruits to the cooled granola. Store in airtight containers.

(For inn information see page 44)

Caramel Apple French Toast

Makes 6 servings.

Every weekend the Whitegate Inn serves this fabulous French toast as its signature Sunday Breakfast. Guests enjoy the lavish presentation that includes hot syrup, fresh fruit, Canadian bacon, and juice.

1 cup packed brown sugar
½ cup (1 stick) butter
2 tablespoons light corn syrup
1 cup chopped pecans
12 slices sweet French bread, cut about ½ inch thick
8 small green apples, peeled, cored, and thinly sliced
6 eggs
1½ cups milk
1 teaspoon vanilla extract
Cinnamon and nutmeg to taste
Hot syrup and whipped cream, optional

Coat a 13x9-inch glass baking dish with nonstick cooking spray. In a small saucepan, combine the brown sugar, butter, and corn syrup. Cook over medium heat, stirring constantly, until the butter is melted and the mixture is well combined and thickened. Pour into the prepared baking dish. Sprinkle with the chopped pecans. Place one layer of the sliced French bread (6 slices) on top of the syrup and pecans. Layer the sliced apples on top of the bread slices. In a blender, combine the eggs, milk, and vanilla. Pour half of the egg/milk mixture over the apples and the first layer of bread. Place the remaining 6 slices of bread on top of the apples, and pour the remaining egg/milk mixture over the top layer of bread. Sprinkle with the cinnamon and nutmeg. Cover with plastic wrap and refrigerate 8 to 10 hours. When ready to cook, preheat the oven to 350°F. Bake for 60 minutes, or until golden brown. To serve, place a double layer of French toast on each of 6 plates. Serve with the whipped cream and hot syrup, if desired.

(For inn information see page 46)

Haydon Street Inn

Originally built in the early 1900s, the Haydon Street Inn is a two-story Queen Anne Victorian residence. A two-story Victorian cottage was added in 1987, giving it the appearance of a storybook house. This intimate bed and breakfast inn is located near California's prime grape-growing regions: Dry Creek, Alexander, and the Russian River Valley. Two guest rooms feature dramatic high dormer ceilings, wide plank pine floors, lovely antiques, and private baths with double whirlpool tubs. They are decorated with handmade rugs, French and American antiques, custom-made down comforters, and designer wall coverings.

A scrumptious country breakfast is served each morning. Afternoon refreshments are served in the parlor.

INNKEEPERS:	*Dick & Pat Bertapelle*
ADDRESS:	*321 Haydon Street*
	Healdsburg, CA 95448
TELEPHONE:	*(707) 433-5228; (800) 528-3703*
E-MAIL:	*innkeeper@haydon.com*
WEBSITE:	*www.haydon.com*
ROOMS:	*8 Rooms; 1 Suite; All with private baths*
CHILDREN:	*Children over the age of 12 are welcome*
ANIMALS:	*Prohibited; Resident dog*

designated areas

Croissant French Toast

Makes 16 servings.

6 eggs
½ cup half-and-half
¾ cup milk
¼ cup cinnamon
¼ cup vanilla extract
16 large croissants
½ cup mascarpone cheese (substitute cream cheese, if desired)
5 cups corn flakes, crushed to make 2 cups
Oil or butter, for griddle
½ cup lemon curd, thinned with a few drops of water
Blueberry syrup (homemade or purchased)
Blueberries, fresh or frozen
Powdered sugar, for garnish
6 large bananas, each cut into 8 (1-inch) pieces
Star fruit, sliced, for garnish
Kiwi, sliced, for garnish
Mint leaves, for garnish
16 strawberries, fanned, for garnish

In a medium bowl, beat the eggs, and combine with the half-and-half, milk, cinnamon, and vanilla. Slit the back of the croissants. Insert a dab of cheese in the slits. Dip the croissants in the egg mixture, soaking briefly. Roll each croissant in the crushed corn flakes, packing on as much as possible. Wrap the croissants in waxed paper, and chill 8 to 10 hours. To cook, oil or butter a griddle, and heat to 350°F. Cook the croissants on the griddle about 5 minutes per side, or until golden brown. While the croissants are cooking, warm the lemon curd, thinning with a little water. Warm the blueberry syrup, adding blueberries during the last few minutes of heating. To serve, dust each plate with powdered sugar. Place 3 banana pieces on each plate, and use them to prop up the croissants. Drape with the berry syrup on one side and the lemon curd on the other. Garnish with the fruits and mint.

Arroyo Village Inn

Located approximately halfway between Los Angeles and San Francisco, the Arroyo Village Inn combines the charm and hospitality of an English inn with the adventure and romance of California's central coast. It is the perfect getaway for romance and total pampering. All rooms have air-conditioning, private baths, queen- or king-size beds, and a comfortable sitting area. Rocking chairs and candles add charm.

Breakfasts are truly memorable at the Arroyo Village Inn. Favorite gourmet delights include country morning frittata, Dutch apple pancakes, Mexican quiche, and blueberry cream cheese coffee cake.

Nearby points of interest include the Edna Valley wine country, Pismo Beach, Lake Lopez, and the Hearst Castle. Seasonal events include the Jazz and Mozart Festivals and the Pismo Clam and Strawberry Festivals.

INNKEEPERS: *Gina, Adriana, and John*
ADDRESS: *407 El Camino Real*
Arroyo Grande, CA 93420
TELEPHONE: *(805) 489-5926; (800) 563-7762*
E-MAIL: *avi@onemain.com*
WEBSITE: *www.arroyovillageinn.com*
ROOMS: *7 Rooms; All with private baths*
CHILDREN: *Unsuitable*
ANIMALS: *Prohibited*

Croissant French Toast
à l'Orange

Makes 6 servings.

The orange marmalade gives this unique French toast a burst of flavor.

6 large croissants, cut into top and bottom halves
1 (9-ounce) jar orange marmalade
3 ounces orange juice
5 eggs
1 cup heavy cream
1 teaspoon almond extract
Strawberries, whole or sliced, for garnish
Fresh mandarin orange sections, for garnish (look for any of these
    members of the mandarin-orange family: clementine, dancy,
    satsuma, or tangerine)
Syrup of choice

Place the bottom halves of the croissants into a 13x9-inch buttered baking dish. In a small bowl, combine the marmalade with the orange juice; mix completely. Spoon the thinned marmalade over each croissant bottom half, saving a little to be used as a glaze for the tops of the croissants. Place the croissant tops over the croissant bottom halves. In a medium bowl, beat together the eggs, cream, and almond extract. Pour this mixture over the croissants. Spoon the remaining marmalade over the top of each croissant as a glaze. Cover the baking dish, and refrigerate 8 to 10 hours, allowing the croissants to soak in the egg mixture. When ready to cook, remove the baking dish from the refrigerator, and allow it to stand at room temperature for 45 to 60 minutes before baking. Preheat the oven to 350°F. Bake, uncovered, for 25 minutes. Serve the croissants hot, garnished with the strawberries and mandarin orange sections. Offer syrup on the side.

Martine Inn

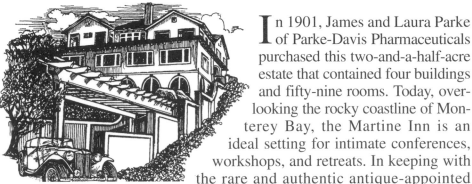

In 1901, James and Laura Parke of Parke-Davis Pharmaceuticals purchased this two-and-a-half-acre estate that contained four buildings and fifty-nine rooms. Today, overlooking the rocky coastline of Monterey Bay, the Martine Inn is an ideal setting for intimate conferences, workshops, and retreats. In keeping with the rare and authentic antique-appointed ambiance, each of the six conference room areas has a unique interior design, different views and varying sizes. Each of the twenty-six guest rooms boasts a private bathroom and authentic museum antiques.

Off-site activities include picnics on the beach, golf, scuba diving, kayaking, bicycling, tennis, historical tours, nature hikes, and day trips to Monterey wine country, Big Sur, and the Hearst Castle.

Meals at the Martine Inn are prepared in a Victorian kitchen and served on Victorian-style china, old Sheffield silver, and antique crystal. In the early evening, wine and hors d'oeuvres are served in the parlor.

INNKEEPER:	*Don Martine*
ADDRESS:	*255 Oceanview Boulevard*
	Pacific Grove, CA 93950
TELEPHONE:	*(831) 373-3388; (800) 852-5588*
E-MAIL:	*don@martineinn.com*
WEBSITE:	*www.martineinn.com*
ROOMS:	*26 Rooms; All with private baths*
CHILDREN:	*Welcome*
ANIMALS:	*Prohibited*

designated areas

Custard Baked French Toast

Makes 6 to 8 servings.

During baking, a custard is formed on the bottom of this satisfying French toast. Incredibly rich—and incredibly delicious.

10 to 12 slices raisin bread, each slice about ½-inch thick
10 eggs, beaten
2 cups sugar
2 tablespoons vanilla extract
5 cups half-and-half
1 tablespoon butter, room temperature
Powdered sugar, fresh berries, fresh mint sprigs, for garnish
Maple or berry syrup, optional

Preheat the oven to 375°F. Coat a 13x9-inch baking pan with nonstick cooking spray. Place a single layer of raisin bread in the pan, using 5 or 6 slices. The number of slices used depends on their size. Use as many as you need to cover the bottom of the pan, cutting slices to fit, if necessary. In a large bowl, combine eggs, sugar, and vanilla. Add the half-and-half, and beat until mixture is blended thoroughly. Ladle some of the custard mixture over the single layer of raisin bread in the baking pan, just until the bread is covered. Butter the remaining slices of bread, one side only. Place a second layer of bread, buttered side up, over the first layer. Ladle the remaining custard mixture over the top of the bread, filling the pan to within one-half-inch from the top. Bake for 45 minutes, or until a knife inserted in the center comes out clean. Let the French toast rest for 10 minutes after removing from the oven. Cut into 6 large portions, or 8 smaller ones, and place on serving plates. Dust with the powdered sugar, sprinkle with the berries, and garnish with the mint. Serve with syrup, if desired.

Foothill House

Nestled among the western foothills north of Calistoga, Foothill House offers exquisite views of Napa Valley and Mount St. Helena. Nature abounds with wildlife such as quail, hummingbirds, and hawks. The cozy, yet spacious rooms are individually decorated with country antiques. The color scheme complements the handmade quilts that adorn the four-poster beds. A cozy fireplace in each room adds warmth and ambiance.

The generous gourmet breakfast features fresh fruit, homemade breads, delectable muffins, and freshly squeezed orange juice. Appetizing hors d'oeuvres and refreshments are served late afternoon.

INNKEEPERS:	*Doris & Gus Beckert*
ADDRESS:	*3037 Foothill Boulevard*
	Calistoga, CA 94515
TELEPHONE:	*(707) 942-6933; (800) 942-6933*
E-MAIL:	*gus@calicom.net*
WEBSITE:	*www.foothillhouse.com*
ROOMS:	*3 Suites; 2 Cottages; All with private baths*
CHILDREN:	*Children over the age of 10 are welcome*
ANIMALS:	*Prohibited; Resident cat*

designated areas

Decadent French Toast Soufflé

Makes 8 servings.

The soufflé mixture must be refrigerated 8 to 10 hours, so this is a great recipe to make when you want a head start on breakfast or brunch.

4 large or 5 medium croissants
2 (3-ounce) packages cream cheese, room temperature
½ cup (1 stick) butter, room temperature
¼ plus ½ cup maple syrup
10 eggs
3 cups half-and-half
Cinnamon

Sauce:
½ cup (1 stick) butter
½ cup maple syrup

Garnish:
Powdered sugar
Chopped pecans
Edible flower or fresh berry

Grease 8 individual (1-cup) soufflé dishes or a 13x9-inch glass baking dish. In a food processor, coarsely chop the croissants. Distribute the coarse crumbs evenly in the prepared dish(es). Using the food processor again, combine the cream cheese, butter, and the ¼ cup maple syrup. Dollop 1 spoonful in each individual soufflé dish in the middle of the croissant crumbs, or dollop 8 spoonfuls evenly spaced if using the large baking dish. In a large bowl, beat together the eggs, half-and-half and the remaining ½ cup maple syrup; pour over the ingredients in the dish(es). Sprinkle with the cinnamon. Cover and refrigerate 8 to 10 hours. When ready to cook, preheat the oven to 350°F. Bake, uncovered, 30 minutes for individual dishes, or 45 to 50 minutes for large baking dish, or until set, puffed, and golden.

To make the sauce, heat the butter and syrup together. Pour over the warm soufflé. Sprinkle with the powdered sugar and pecans. Garnish with a flower or berry.

Fluffy Vanilla & Cinnamon French Toast with Bananas & Almonds

Makes 6 servings.

6 large eggs
1 cup low-fat milk
¾ teaspoon vanilla extract
1 teaspoon cinnamon
12 slices sourdough French bread (cut ½- to 1-inch thick)
Butter or margarine, for griddle
6 bananas, for topping
Powdered sugar, for garnish
¼ cup finely chopped almonds, for garnish
Syrup, for serving

Get out a rimmed, large baking sheet. In a large bowl, mix together the eggs, milk, vanilla, and cinnamon until light and frothy. Dip the bread slices thoroughly in the egg/milk mixture, and place on the baking sheet. Pour any leftover mixture over the bread slices. Cover and refrigerate 8 to 10 hours. When ready to cook, heat a griddle to medium, and melt about 1 tablespoon of butter or margarine on the griddle. Cook the bread slices on one side until light brown and crispy. Turn the slices over, and brown the other side. To serve, place 2 pieces of the French toast on each of 6 plates. Slice a banana over the top of each serving. Sprinkle with the powdered sugar, and garnish with the chopped almonds. Serve hot with syrup.

(For inn information see page 30)

Homemade Granola

Makes about 14 cups granola.

5 cups rolled oats (old-fashioned or quick-cooking)
1 cup sliced almonds
1 cup chopped walnuts
1 cup chopped pecans
1 cup sesame seeds
1 cup wheat germ
1 cup shredded coconut
1 cup unsalted sunflower seeds
1 cup safflower oil
1 cup honey
1 cup raisins
1 cup currants

Preheat the oven to 325°F. Lightly oil a rimmed baking sheet. In a very large bowl, combine the oats, almonds, walnuts, pecans, sesame seeds, wheat germ, coconut, and sunflower seeds. In a small saucepan, on medium-low, heat the oil and honey together until well combined. Pour the warm oil/honey mixture over the dry ingredients in the bowl; mix well. Spread the mixture onto the prepared baking sheet. Bake for approximately 20 minutes. Let the granola cool on the baking sheet, and then add the raisins and currants (or any other dried fruit of choice). Store the granola in an airtight container.

Note: This recipe makes a large quantity. For long-term storage, the granola should be refrigerated or frozen to maintain its freshness.

> **Carol's Corner**
> *Try creating your own special version of homemade granola by adding your favorite dried fruits to the mix—chopped dried apricots, dried cranberries, or dried cherries are all excellent, colorful additions.*

(For inn information see page 72)

Gables Inn

Completed in 1877, the Gables Inn is a near-perfect example of high Victorian Gothic revival architecture. Boasting graceful twelve-foot ceilings, three Italian marble fireplaces, and a spectacular mahogany spiral staircase, the most striking detail is the source of its name: the fifteen gables crowning the unusual keyhole-shaped windows. Each bedroom is distinctly appointed with tasteful antique furnishings.

Local points of interest include San Luis Obispo's 1772 historic mission, the Hearst Castle, cliffs of Montana de Oro, Morro Bay, Pismo Beach, and the majestic hills and lush vineyards of Edna Valley.

Within a short drive, guests have easy access to river rafting, fishing, early morning hot air balloon rides, antique shopping, and over 150 wineries.

Breakfast at the Gables Inn is served in the lovely formal dining room. Always fresh and homemade, breakfast items include juice, fruits in season, an ever-changing entrée, breads and pastries, coffee, and a selection of fine teas.

INNKEEPERS:	*Mike & Judy Ogne*
ADDRESS:	*4257 Petaluma Hill Road*
	Santa Rosa, CA 95404
TELEPHONE:	*(707) 585-7777; (800) GABLES N*
E-MAIL:	*innkeeper@thegablesinn.com*
WEBSITE:	*www.thegablesinn.com*
ROOMS:	*7 Rooms; 1 Cottage; All with private baths*
CHILDREN:	*Children over the age of 12 are welcome*
ANIMALS:	*Prohibited*

Judy's French Toast with Fruit Syrup

Makes 4 to 6 servings.

6 slices French bread (cut 1- to 1½-inches thick)
1 cup whole milk or half-and-half
4 eggs
1 teaspoon vanilla extract
1 tablespoon sugar
1 to 2 tablespoons butter, for griddle
Fruit Syrup, for serving (recipe on page 142)

Place the bread slices on a rimmed cookie sheet. Using a blender, combine the milk (or half-and-half), eggs, vanilla, and sugar. Pour the milk/egg mixture over the bread slices. Cover and refrigerate at least an hour or two before cooking to let the bread absorb all of the milk/egg mixture. To cook the French toast, heat a griddle to medium-hot, and melt the butter on the griddle. Cook the bread slices on one side until golden brown. Turn the slices over; reduce the heat to low. Let the bread cook slowly for several minutes until cooked through and the bottom side is golden brown. To serve, place the French toast on warmed plates, and top with the warm Fruit Syrup (recipe on page 142).

North Coast Country Inn

The North Coast Country Inn is a cluster of weathered rustic buildings that overlooks the beautiful Mendocino Coast. Nestled in a redwood and pine forest, this distinguished inn boasts six suites carefully furnished with authentic antiques, handmade quilts, and king- or queen-size beds.

The property was once part of a coastal sheep ranch. Fruit trees still flourish in the lower garden, all that remains of the old ranch orchard.

INNKEEPERS: *Maureen Topping & Bill Shupe*
ADDRESS: *34591 South Highway 1*
Gualala, CA 95445
TELEPHONE: *(707) 884-4537; (800) 959-4537*
E-MAIL: *ncci@mcn.org*
WEBSITE: *www.northcoastcountryinn.com*
ROOMS: *6 Suites; All with private baths*
CHILDREN: *Unsuitable*
ANIMALS: *Prohibited; Resident dog and cat*

designated areas

call first

"Thank you for a lovely quiet retreat from the chaos and insanity of the rest of the world." —Guest, North Coast Country Inn

Overnight Praline French Toast

Makes 6 servings.

1 cup packed brown sugar
½ cup (1 stick) butter
2 tablespoons light corn syrup
½ to 1 cup pecans, coarsely chopped
12 slices white sandwich bread
6 eggs
1½ cups milk
1 teaspoon rum extract
¼ teaspoon salt
Cinnamon
Syrup, optional
Whipped cream, optional

Lightly coat a 13x9-inch baking dish with nonstick cooking spray. In a small saucepan, combine the brown sugar, butter and corn syrup. Cook over medium heat until bubbling and thickened, stirring constantly. Pour the syrup mixture into the prepared baking dish. Sprinkle the pecans evenly over the syrup mixture. Place 6 slices of bread on top of the pecans and syrup mixture; then top those slices with the 6 remaining slices of bread. In a large bowl, beat the eggs. Combine the beaten eggs with the milk, rum extract, and salt, blending well. Pour the egg mixture evenly over the bread slices. Sprinkle cinnamon over the top. Cover and chill overnight. Preheat the oven to 350°F. When ready to cook, bake, uncovered, for 40 to 45 minutes, or until lightly browned. Serve immediately with the syrup and a dollop of the whipped cream, if desired.

Carol's Corner
What if breakfast is ready, but your guests aren't? The North Coast Country Inn has been successful holding this fabulous French toast on a warming tray for up to 2 hours.

Cavanagh Inn

Historic Petaluma is home to the Cavanagh Inn bed and breakfast. This elegant home is one of the grand Victorian homes that survived the ravages of the 1906 San Francisco earthquake. As Sonoma County's southern most city, this riverfront Victorian town is only thirty-two miles north of San Francisco. The inn's décor is formal Victorian, and all the rooms are exquisitely decorated. The cottage, also part of the inn, is decorated with a casual garden theme, complete with a garden mural on the upstairs landing.

The award-winning culinary skills of chef Jeanne Farris are showcased each morning. A typical breakfast menu might include homemade granola with yogurt and fresh seasonal fruit, overnight French toast, and tasty cardamom pears.

INNKEEPERS:	*Ray & Jeanne Farris*
ADDRESS:	*10 Keller Street*
	Petaluma, CA 94952
TELEPHONE:	*(707) 765-4657; (888) 765-4658*
E-MAIL:	*info@cavanaghinn.com*
WEBSITE:	*www.cavanaghinn.com*
ROOMS:	*7 Rooms; Five with private baths; Two shared baths*
CHILDREN:	*Children over the age of 12 are welcome*
ANIMALS:	*Prohibited; Resident cat*

Panettone French Toast

Makes 6 large or 12 small servings.

1½ cups packed brown sugar
1 cup (2 sticks) butter
4 tablespoons corn syrup
1 (1-pound) box panettone
   Italian bread (see Carol's
   Corner)
10 large eggs

3½ cups milk
¼ cup Grand Marnier
   (orange-flavored liqueur)
Powdered sugar, for garnish
Whipped cream, for garnish
Fresh fruit, for garnish

Coat a 15x10-inch baking dish with nonstick cooking spray. In a micro-wavable bowl, combine the brown sugar, butter, and corn syrup. Heat in the microwave until the butter is melted; whisk until the brown sugar, butter, and corn syrup are well combined. Pour this mixture into the pre-pared baking dish. Remove the loaf of bread from its packaging, making sure to peel all paper from the loaf. Cut the loaf into 6 thick, evenly sliced pieces of bread. Place the slices in the baking dish, covering all the brown sugar mixture. (If necessary, trim the 6 slices to fit the baking dish, using any extra small pieces to fill the spaces between slices.) In a large bowl, beat the eggs with the milk and Grand Marnier until well mixed. Pour the mixture evenly over the bread. Refrigerate covered 8 to 10 hours. When ready to cook, preheat the oven to 350°F. Bake uncovered for approxi-mately 55 minutes or until lightly browned and puffed (the French toast will deflate when removed from the oven). Cut into serving portions. When placing the French toast on each serving plate, be sure to scoop up some of the hot caramel from the bottom of the baking dish. Dust with the powdered sugar. Top with the whipped cream, and garnish with the fresh fruit.

Carol's Corner

Panettone (pan-uh-TOH-nee) is an Italian sweet bread traditionally served at Christmastime. It is baked in a tall, cylindrical shape, and contains raisins, candied citrus peel, and sometimes nuts or other dried fruit. Look for it around the holidays, packaged in an attractive box, at specialty food markets. It can also be ordered through some food catalogs, and it is sometimes available from Italian restaurants.

Arbor House Oven Omelet
Artichoke Soufflé
Baked Lemon Eggs
Baked Quesadilla Squares
Baked Vegetable Quiche
Bella Torta
Cheese Soufflé
Cottage Cheese Soufflé
Crustless Potato Cheese Pie
Gerstle Park Inn Egg Casserole
Green Chile & Cheese Egg Casserole
Hash Brown Quiche
Italian Sausage Frittata
Miss Amy's Favorite Vegetable Frittata
Monterey Eggs & Salsa
Ham & Asparagus Strata
Mushroom Crust Quiche
Santa Clara Quiche
Sonoma Green Chile Eggs
Fresh Vegetable Frittata
Sourdough Egg Casserole
South of the Border Crustless Quiche
Spinach Quiche

Egg Entrées

Arbor House Inn

Surrounded by lovely outdoor gardens, the Arbor House Inn bed and breakfast is located just one block from Clear Lake, California's largest and oldest natural lake. All guest rooms have outdoor porches with private entrances. Guests may also enjoy a Jacuzzi in their private bathrooms or the outdoor spa that is surrounded by English cottage gardens and a small Koi pond. Local restaurants, shops, and a public boat ramp are within walking distance.

Guests enjoy an appetizing three-course breakfast that includes a special daily entrée, fruit, baked goodies, juice, and freshly ground coffee. In the evening, the inn serves Lake County wine with cheese and crackers or sourdough bread in the dining room.

INNKEEPER:	*Lori Bacci*
ADDRESS:	*150 Clear Lake Avenue*
	Lakeport, CA 95453
TELEPHONE:	*(707) 263-6444*
E-MAIL:	*arborinn@pacific.net*
WEBSITE:	*www.arborhousebnb.com*
ROOMS:	*4 Rooms; 1 Suite; All with private baths*
CHILDREN:	*Welcome*
ANIMALS:	*Prohibited*

designated areas

Arbor House Oven Omelet

Makes 6 to 8 servings.

12 large eggs
1¼ cups half-and-half
1 tablespoon bacon drippings (save when bacon is cooking)
1 pound sliced bacon, cooked and crumbled into bite-size pieces
1 bunch green onions, chopped (white and green parts)
3 cups shredded pepper jack cheese
½ teaspoon black pepper
2 dashes cayenne pepper

Preheat the oven to 350°F. Grease an 11x2-inch round baking dish. In a large bowl, beat the eggs with a whisk or mixer. Add the half-and-half and bacon drippings. Mix well. Stir in the cooked bacon, green onions, cheese, and the black and cayenne peppers. Pour the mixture into the prepared baking dish. Bake, uncovered, for 40 to 50 minutes, or until the center is puffed and golden brown. Let the omelet stand for 5 to 10 minutes before cutting into serving pieces.

Make-ahead tip: To save time in the morning, precook the bacon (remember to reserve one tablespoon bacon drippings for the omelet), chop the green onions, and grate the cheese.

Artichoke Soufflé

Makes 1 large serving.

This recipe is easily modified when you are cooking for more than one person. Multiply the ingredients by the number of people you are serving.

¼ cup canned artichoke hearts, rinsed and drained
3 eggs
Splash of buttermilk (about 2 teaspoons)
Salt and pepper
⅛ cup (about 2 tablespoons) grated pepper jack cheese

Preheat the oven to 375°F. Coat a 6-ounce ramekin (individual baking dish) with nonstick cooking spray. Chop the artichokes into small pieces. In a large bowl, combine the eggs and buttermilk. Using a mixer, beat just until frothy. Stir in the artichoke pieces and the salt and pepper to taste. Put the cheese in the bottom of the ramekin. Pour the egg mixture over the cheese. (The ramekin will be nearly full.) Bake for about 20 to 23 minutes, or until the soufflé pops out over the top of the ramekin and is golden brown.

(For inn information see page 52)

Baked Lemon Eggs

Makes 4 servings.

The addition of Gouda cheese and lemon zest adds extra flavor to this classic egg dish.

8 tablespoons (½ cup) heavy whipping cream
1½ teaspoons finely grated lemon peel (zest)
½ cup grated Gouda cheese
4 eggs
Salt and pepper
2 tablespoons chopped fresh parsley

Preheat the oven to 350°F. Liberally butter 4 small (individual serving-size) baking dishes. Pour 1 tablespoon of the cream into each dish, and sprinkle the lemon zest equally over the cream. Sprinkle the grated cheese equally over the lemon zest and cream. Gently break an egg into each dish. Add the salt and pepper to taste. Pour another tablespoon of cream over each egg, and top with the chopped parsley. Bake for 12 to 15 minutes, or until the eggs are just set.

(For inn information see page 72)

Baked Quesadilla Squares

Makes 6 servings.

2 cups shredded Cheddar cheese
2 cups shredded Monterey Jack cheese
2 (4-ounce) cans diced mild green chiles
4 eggs
2 cups milk
1½ cups baking mix (such as Bisquick)
½ cup salsa
Sour cream, optional
Guacamole, optional
Salsa, optional

Preheat the oven to 425°F. Coat a 13x9-inch baking dish with nonstick cooking spray. Sprinkle the two kinds of cheese into the bottom of the dish; mix together. Top with the green chiles. In a large bowl, beat the eggs. Combine the beaten eggs with the milk and baking mix, beating until smooth. Carefully pour this mixture over the cheese and chiles. Top with the salsa. Bake for 25 to 30 minutes until puffed and golden. Cool for 10 minutes. Cut into squares and serve. Let your guests add optional toppings.

(For inn information see page 100)

Baked Vegetable Quiche

Makes 6 to 8 servings.

1 cup fresh chopped vegetables (zucchini, red pepper, mushroom,
    broccoli, asparagus . . .)
1 medium onion, minced
1 (14.5-ounce) can cream of broccoli, mushroom, or asparagus soup
¼ cup milk
4 eggs
2 tablespoons bread crumbs
½ cup shredded cheese (Cheddar, Swiss, or mozzarella)
1 frozen 9-inch deep-dish pie crust

Preheat the oven to 350°F. Sauté fresh vegetables and onion in a small
amount of oil until soft, and set aside. Mix together the undiluted soup,
milk, and eggs until smooth. Add the bread crumbs, cheese, and vegetables
and mix well. Pour the mixture into the frozen pie crust and bake until
golden brown (around 1 hour). Let the quiche stand for 10 minutes before
cutting.

(For inn information see page 210)

Ink House

Located in the midst of Napa Valley's wine growing region, the Ink House bed and breakfast is a grand and historic landmark home. The glass-enclosed observatory is its most distinctive architectural feature. Perched fifty feet above the valley floor, the Scottish stained glass windows enhance the 12x20-foot observatory where guests read, sip wine, nap, or watch the sunset. This Italianate Victorian offers two first-floor parlors that contain a concert grand piano, fireplace, circa 1870 pump organ, and crystal chandeliers. This landmark home was the site of the 1960 filming of Elvis Presley's film *Wild in the Country*.

Many afternoons, local wine makers share their wine and wine-making secrets with guests.

INNKEEPER:	*Diane DeFilipi*
ADDRESS:	*1575 St. Helena Hwy*
	St. Helena, CA 94574
TELEPHONE:	*(707) 963-3890*
E-MAIL:	*inkhousebb@aol.com*
WEBSITE:	*www.inkhouse.com*
ROOMS:	*7 Rooms; Private and shared baths*
CHILDREN:	*Welcome*
ANIMALS:	*Prohibited*

designated areas

Bella Torta

Makes 15 servings.

4 (10-ounce) boxes frozen
chopped spinach
4 plus 12 eggs
1 cup soft bread crumbs
½ teaspoon ground nutmeg
⅔ cup cream or half-and-half
⅓ cup pine nuts
2 tablespoons butter
1 cup milk
1 teaspoon Italian seasoning

1½ cups sun-dried tomatoes,
chopped (drain or blot excess
oil)
4 ounces (1 cup) provolone
cheese, thinly sliced or
shredded
½ teaspoon freshly grated black
pepper
15 marinated artichoke hearts

Coat a 13x9-inch glass baking dish with nonstick cooking spray. Cook the spinach according to package directions and cool. Completely drain all moisture from the spinach, squeezing with your hands. Preheat the oven to 350°F. In a large bowl, beat the 4 eggs. Add the cooked and drained spinach, bread crumbs, nutmeg, cream, and pine nuts. In a large skillet over low heat, melt the butter. Meanwhile, in a large bowl, beat the remaining 12 eggs with the milk and Italian seasoning. Add the egg mixture to the skillet to make scrambled eggs, but don't cook completely. (The eggs need to stay very moist, since they will cook more during baking.) Spread the undercooked eggs evenly into the bottom of the prepared baking dish. Sprinkle the sun-dried tomatoes over the eggs. Top the sun-dried tomatoes with the provolone cheese. Layer the spinach mixture on top of the cheese. Sprinkle with the pepper. Place the artichokes evenly in 3 rows of 5 artichokes each. Bake, uncovered, for 40 minutes. Cool for 5 minutes; cut into squares.

Make-ahead tip: May be prepared one day ahead of time and stored in a tightly covered dish in the refrigerator before baking.

Cheese Soufflé

Makes 6 to 9 servings.

An excellent, easy do-ahead egg and cheese dish. If you don't have a soufflé dish, a 9-inch casserole dish may be used instead.

8 slices (about ¾-inch thick) day-old French bread
1 cup (4 ounces) shredded Swiss or Jarlsberg cheese
6 eggs, beaten
2½ cups milk
¼ cup (½ stick) butter, melted and cooled slightly
½ teaspoon dry ground mustard
Salt and pepper

Lightly coat a 9-inch soufflé dish with nonstick cooking spray or butter. Remove the crusts from the bread, and cut bread into 1-inch squares. Place the bread pieces, along with the shredded cheese, in the soufflé dish, and toss together to combine. In a large bowl, mix together the beaten eggs, milk, melted butter, dry mustard, and salt and pepper to taste. Pour the egg/milk mixture over the bread and cheese. Cover and refrigerate 8 to 10 hours. When ready to cook, preheat the oven to 325°F. Bake for 1 hour, until the soufflé is puffed and lightly browned. (The soufflé is done when a knife inserted near the center comes out clean.)

"Such peace and tranquility. We return each year to refresh our souls."
—Guest, Mangels House

(For inn information see page 50)

Cottage Cheese Soufflé

Makes 6 large or 9 small servings.

A cheese lover's delight. The cottage cheese melts and mingles with the shredded Monterey Jack (or Swiss cheese) as the soufflé bakes. This is a very rich, melt-in-your-mouth egg dish.

2 cups (8 ounces) shredded Monterey Jack or Swiss cheese
1 cup milk
1 cup all-purpose flour
1 pint (16 ounces) low-fat cottage cheese, small curd
6 large eggs (or egg substitute equivalent)
½ cup (1 stick) butter or margarine, melted
Chopped parsley, for garnish

Preheat the oven to 350°F. Coat a 9x9-inch square baking pan with nonstick cooking spray. Sprinkle the shredded cheese evenly onto the bottom of the pan. In a large bowl, combine the milk, flour, cottage cheese, eggs, and melted butter (or margarine). Whisk together until thoroughly mixed. Pour the mixture into the pan over the shredded cheese. Sprinkle the chopped parsley evenly over the top before baking. Bake for 45 minutes or until lightly browned. Let the soufflé stand for just a few minutes, and then cut into serving portions.

(For inn information see page 62)

Raford House

B uilt in the 1880s, the Raford House originally overlooked a valley of hops. Today, the historic landmark is surrounded by towering palm trees and old-fashioned flower gardens and overlooks lush vineyards. Each guest room is uniquely and tastefully furnished.

This charming Victorian is minutes from Sonoma County's award-winning wineries and a short drive to beautiful, old-fashioned Healdsburg Square with its antique shops, boutiques, bakeries, and restaurants.

Begin the day with a hearty country breakfast prepared by your hosts and served in the beautifully decorated turn-of-the-century style dining room.

INNKEEPERS:	*Carole & Jack Vore*
ADDRESS:	*10630 Wohler Road*
	Healdsburg, CA 95448
TELEPHONE:	*(707) 887-9573; (800) 887-9503*
E-MAIL:	*rafordbb@aol.com*
WEBSITE:	*www.rafordhouse.com*
ROOMS:	*6 Rooms; All with private baths*
CHILDREN:	*Adult children are welcome (Call ahead)*
ANIMALS:	*Prohibited; Resident cat*

designated areas

Crustless Potato Cheese Pie

Makes 5 to 6 servings.

For variety, substitute chopped green onions for the green chiles, or add ham with (or without) chopped red and yellow peppers. Just remember that the recipe below completely fills a 9-inch pie plate. If you are going to add ingredients, use a 10-inch pie plate.

Pie:
6 eggs
½ cup sour cream
Hot pepper sauce to taste (Raford House uses 4 to 5 dashes)
¼ teaspoon salt
1 (4-ounce) can diced green chiles
3 cups frozen hash brown potatoes, thawed
1 cup (4 ounces) shredded Cheddar cheese
Paprika

Topping:
1 medium tomato, thinly sliced into 5 to 6 slices
½ pound (about 7 to 8 slices) bacon, crisply cooked and crumbled
¼ cup shredded Cheddar cheese
Parsley, for garnish, optional

Preheat the oven to 350°F. Coat a 9-inch pie plate (or 10-inch if using additional ingredients) with nonstick cooking spray. In a large bowl, beat together the eggs, sour cream, hot pepper sauce, and salt. Add the green chiles, thawed hash brown potatoes, and the 1 cup of Cheddar cheese; mix well. Pour the eggs/potato mixture into the prepared pie plate. Sprinkle with the paprika. Bake for 40 to 45 minutes. Remove from the oven. Lay 5 or 6 thin slices of the tomato edge-to-edge arranged in a circle on top of the pie (the number of slices depends on the number of wedges you are serving—each piece should be topped with a tomato slice). Sprinkle with the crumbled bacon and the ¼ cup of Cheddar cheese. Return the pie to the oven, and bake an additional 10 minutes. Let the pie stand for 5 minutes before serving. Garnish each serving with the parsley, if desired.

Gerstle Park Inn
Egg Casserole

Makes 8 large or 12 small servings.

Gerstle Park Inn suggests serving this breakfast dish with homemade salsa and crispy bacon slices, garnishing with fresh herbs, nasturtium blossoms, cherry tomatoes, avocado, or orange slices.

10 eggs
4 cups (16 ounces) grated Monterey Jack cheese
1 pint (16 ounces) small-curd cottage cheese
½ cup (1 stick) butter, melted
½ cup all-purpose flour
1 teaspoon baking powder
½ teaspoon salt
2 (4-ounce) cans chopped green chiles
1 (4-ounce) can sliced black olives
Sliced canned mushrooms, optional
Chopped fresh spinach, optional
Chopped fresh zucchini, optional
Salsa, for topping
Fresh herbs, for garnish
Edible flowers, for garnish
Cherry tomatoes, for garnish
Avocado slices, for garnish
Fresh fruit slices, for garnish

Preheat the oven to 350°F. Coat a 13x9-inch glass baking dish with nonstick cooking spray. In a large bowl, beat the eggs. Add the Monterey Jack and cottage cheeses, melted butter, flour, baking powder, and salt. Mix well. Stir in the chiles, olives, and any optional ingredients, if desired. Spoon the mixture into the prepared baking dish. Bake for 35 to 40 minutes, or until a knife inserted comes out clean. Let stand for 5 minutes on a wire rack. Cut into serving pieces, and top with the salsa. Garnish as desired.

(For inn information see page 74)

Green Chile & Cheese Egg Casserole

Makes 8 servings.

6 eggs
⅜ cup all-purpose flour
¾ teaspoon baking powder
¾ teaspoon dry mustard
1½ cups grated Monterey Jack cheese
1½ cups grated Cheddar cheese
1½ cups small-curd cottage cheese
1 (20-ounce) can chopped mild green chiles, well drained
Sour cream, for garnish
Chopped black olives, for garnish

Preheat the oven to 350°F. Coat a 13x9-inch baking dish with nonstick cooking spray or butter. In a large bowl, whisk or beat the eggs. Sift in the flour, baking powder, and dry mustard. Mix well. Stir in the three cheeses and the green chiles. Pour into the prepared baking dish. Bake for approximately 45 to 50 minutes, or until the casserole is set and lightly browned. Let stand for about 5 minutes before cutting into serving pieces. Garnish with the sour cream and chopped black olives.

Carol's Corner

Dry mustard is a powder derived from finely ground mustard seed. It is used as a seasoning in sauces, egg and cheese dishes, main dishes and salad dressings. You will find it in the spice section of your supermarket. It comes in glass spice bottles or small spice cans.

(For inn information see page 78)

Belle de Jour Inn

Originally built in the late 1870s, the Belle De Jour Inn is located in the heart of California's premium wine country. Situated on a hilltop, encompassed by six acres, the single-story Italianate farmhouse is the residence of the innkeepers. The inn's five cottages provide the perfect romantic hideaway.

Amenities include sun-dried sheets, robes, fresh flowers, air-conditioning, refrigerators, and ceiling fans. Allergy sufferers may call ahead to request special accommodations.

Guests are invited each morning to share a bountiful breakfast in the warmth of their country kitchen.

INNKEEPERS: *Tom & Brenda Hearn*
ADDRESS: *16276 Healdsburg Avenue*
Healdsburg, CA 95448
TELEPHONE: *(707) 431-9777*
E-MAIL: *Not Available*
WEBSITE: *www.belledejourinn.com*
ROOMS: *5 Cottages; All with private baths*
CHILDREN: *Unsuitable*
ANIMALS: *Prohibited; Resident cat*

Hash Brown Quiche

Makes 8 to 10 servings.

This is a very user-friendly, basic recipe that is easily varied to use ingredients that you have on hand, or to suit your own personal taste. A warm basket of muffins, melon slices, and breakfast sausage would be welcome additions to this brunch entrée.

1 (26-ounce) package frozen shredded hash browns, thawed
1½ cups shredded Monterey Jack cheese
3 eggs
1 teaspoon salt
¼ teaspoon white pepper
Milk (about ¼ to ⅓ cup)

Preheat the oven to 425°F. Coat a 10-inch round baking dish with nonstick cooking spray. Pour the thawed hash browns into the prepared dish. The dish will be full. Level the potatoes (don't heap them in the middle). Bake the hash browns until lightly browned, about 30 minutes. Remove from the oven. Sprinkle the shredded cheese over the top of the browned potatoes. In a large measuring cup, whisk together the eggs, salt, white pepper, and enough milk to make 1 cup liquid. Pour the egg/milk mixture over the potatoes and cheese. Reduce the oven temperature to 350°F. Bake for approximately 30 minutes longer, or until the cheese is melted and golden. Remove from the oven, and let the quiche stand for 10 minutes. Slice into serving pieces.

Variation: Add crumbled bacon, fresh herbs, chopped vegetables, or use a different kind of cheese.

Italian Sausage Frittata

Makes 8 servings.

1½ pounds mild Italian bulk sausage
Garlic powder
2 tablespoons butter or margarine
¼ cup white wine
3 cups (about 8 ounces) sliced fresh mushrooms
3 large Swiss chard leaves, cut into thin strips
1 cup grated mild Cheddar cheese
9 eggs
1¼ cups milk
2 to 3 tablespoons Dijon mustard
Sour cream, for topping
Salsa, for topping
Chopped chives, for garnish

Preheat the oven to 350°F. Coat a 13x9-inch glass baking dish with nonstick cooking spray. In a large skillet, brown the sausage; drain. Spread the sausage evenly in the prepared baking dish; sprinkle lightly with the garlic powder. In a large sauté pan, melt the butter, and add the wine. Add the mushrooms, and sauté until almost all of the liquid is absorbed or evaporated. Spoon the mushrooms over the sausage. Top with the Swiss chard and grated cheese. In a large bowl, beat together the eggs, milk, and Dijon mustard. Pour this mixture evenly over all ingredients in the baking dish. Bake, uncovered, for 50 to 60 minutes, or until the middle of the frittata is firm to the touch. Remove from the oven, and let stand 15 minutes before cutting. Serve with the sour cream and salsa. Garnish with the chopped chives, if desired.

(For inn information see page 78)

Miss Amy's Favorite Vegetable Frittata

Makes 12 servings.

1 bunch broccoli, cut into bite-size pieces
2 tablespoons butter
1 onion, cut in half, then sliced
1 red pepper, cut into strips
1 pound fresh mushrooms, sliced
18 eggs
1 pint (2 cups) cottage cheese, small curd
4 cups shredded cheese (Cheddar and mozzarella mixture)
¾ cup all-purpose flour
1½ teaspoons baking powder
1 teaspoon garlic salt
Cheese sauce (purchased or homemade) or sour cream, for topping
Tomato slices, for garnish

Steam the broccoli, or heat in a microwave oven for 5 or 6 minutes until just barely tender; do not overcook. Drain off any liquid. In a large sauté pan, melt the butter over medium heat. Cook the onion and pepper until the onion becomes translucent. Add the mushrooms; cook until the liquid produced by the mushrooms is evaporated. In a very large bowl, beat the eggs. Add the cottage cheese, shredded cheese, flour, baking powder, and garlic salt. Mix until well combined. Fold in the broccoli and sautéed vegetables. Preheat the oven to 350°F. Generously grease a 13x9-inch glass baking dish. Pour the mixture into the dish, and bake for approximately 75 minutes, or until the frittata is set and lightly browned. Let cool for 10 to 15 minutes before cutting into serving pieces. Top with the cheese sauce or sour cream. Garnish with fresh tomato slices.

Note: If you prefer, the frittata can be baked in 2 quiche dishes (10 inches). Reduce the baking time to 55 to 60 minutes.

(For inn information see page 98)

Monterey Eggs & Salsa

Makes 12 to 14 individual servings.

Eggs:

2 cups Monterey Jack cheese, shredded

2 cups Cheddar cheese, shredded

1 (8-ounce) carton small-curd cottage cheese

1 (4-ounce) can diced green chiles, drained

1 (4-ounce) jar diced pimientos, drained

10 eggs, beaten

½ cup all-purpose flour

1 teaspoon baking powder

Salsa, for serving (recipe below)

Preheat the oven to 350°F. Generously grease 12 to 14 muffin cups or individual ramekins (about ½-cup capacity). In a large bowl, combine the Monterey Jack, Cheddar, and cottage cheeses, chopped green chiles, and diced pimientos. Add the beaten eggs and mix well. In a small bowl, mix the flour and baking powder; add to the egg/cheese mixture, and blend completely. Spoon the mixture (about one-third cupful) into each of the prepared muffin cups or ramekins, filling them about three-fourths full. Bake for approximately 25 minutes, or until puffed and golden. Serve with the homemade salsa.

Salsa:

½ cup canned, diced green chiles

8 tomatoes, peeled and chopped

1 medium red onion, minced

2 bunches cilantro, chopped

1 teaspoon crushed dried oregano

Salt and pepper

In a large bowl, combine the chiles, tomatoes, onion, cilantro, oregano, and salt and pepper to taste. Mix thoroughly. May be served immediately over the Monterey Eggs, or may be made earlier in the day and refrigerated until ready to serve.

(For inn information see page 92)

Ham & Asparagus Strata

Makes about 8 servings.

12 slices sourdough or French bread
2 cups (or more) shredded Cheddar cheese (or Cheddar/Monterey
  Jack mixture)
1½ cups diced ham or turkey ham, diced
1 pound fresh or canned asparagus, cut into 1-inch pieces (if using
  fresh, steam asparagus for 2 to 4 minutes)
7 eggs
3 cups milk
2 tablespoons minced instant onion
2 teaspoons dry ground mustard
1 teaspoon salt

Generously grease a 13x9-inch baking dish with butter. Remove the crust from the bread slices; cut the slices into 1-inch cubes. Place the bread cubes in two layers on the bottom of the prepared dish. Sprinkle the bread cubes with half the cheese. Layer with the diced ham, asparagus, and the remaining cheese. Beat together the eggs, milk, onion, dry mustard, and salt. Pour the egg/milk mixture over the ingredients in the dish. Cover and refrigerate for 8 to 10 hours. When ready to cook, preheat the oven to 350°. Bake, uncovered, for 50 minutes, or until the top is lightly browned. Let the dish stand for about 10 minutes before cutting into serving pieces.

(For inn information see page 18)

Joshua Grindle Inn

The Joshua Grindle Inn is set on a two-acre estate with views overlooking the Pacific Ocean and Mendocino Bay. Delightful and romantic, the inn offers ten exquisite rooms, five in the Victorian House, two in the Saltbox Cottage, and three in the historic Watertower. Some provide views of Mendocino and the ocean, while others feature wood-burning fireplaces. All the beautifully furnished rooms have private bathrooms. Amenities include luxurious bathrobes, quality toiletries, Mendocino Cookie Company cookies, and Husch wine. This lovely nineteenth-century ocean-view home is an easy walk to unique shops and restaurants.

A satisfying full breakfast is served each morning on an 1830s pine harvest table. Delectable fresh fruit, just-baked muffins, scones, and coffee cake set the tone. A special quiche or frittata, cereal, granola, or yogurt follows.

INNKEEPERS:	*Jim & Arlene Moorehead*
ADDRESS:	*44800 Little Lake Road*
	Mendocino, CA 95460
TELEPHONE:	*(707) 937-4143; (800) GRINDLE*
E-MAIL:	*stay@joshgrin.com*
WEBSITE:	*www.joshgrin.com*
ROOMS:	*10 Rooms; All with private baths*
CHILDREN:	*Children over the age of 12 are welcome*
ANIMALS:	*Prohibited; Resident cats*

Mushroom Crust Quiche

Makes 5 servings.

Chopped sautéed mushrooms, along with crushed saltine crackers, are the basis for the unusual quiche crust.

3 tablespoons butter
8 ounces mushrooms, chopped
½ cup (about 15) saltine crackers, finely crushed
½ cup chopped green onions
½ cup shredded Cheddar cheese
1½ cups small-curd cottage cheese
5 eggs
¼ teaspoon cayenne pepper
¼ teaspoon paprika

Preheat the oven to 350°F. Coat a 9-inch pie plate with nonstick cooking spray. In a medium sauté pan, melt the butter over medium heat. Add the chopped mushrooms and cook until limp and tender. Do not drain; stir in the crushed crackers. Spoon the mushroom mixture into the prepared pie plate. Press the mixture evenly over the bottom and sides to make a crust. Sprinkle the chopped green onions over the mushroom crust. Sprinkle with the shredded cheese. In a food processor, blend the cottage cheese, eggs, and cayenne pepper until smooth. Pour the egg mixture into the crust. Sprinkle with the paprika. Bake for 40 to 50 minutes, or until a knife inserted in the center comes out clean. Let the quiche stand 10 minutes on a wire rack before cutting into serving pieces.

Garden Street Inn

Individual themes, charming antiques, and touches of whimsy characterize the guest rooms and suites of the Garden Street Inn. This award-winning, restored 1887 Italianate Queen Anne Victorian is located in the heart of beautiful San Luis Obispo. Classic décor reflects Victorian charm in the guest rooms. They all have private baths and are appointed with fireplaces, hot tubs, and historical, cultural, and personal memorabilia. Spacious outside decks and a well-stocked library add to the guests' enjoyment.

A bountiful homemade breakfast is served each morning in the McCaffrey morning room. Original stained glass windows help create a joyful tone.

INNKEEPERS: *Steve & Lynn Clements*
ADDRESS: *1212 Garden Street*
San Luis Obispo, CA 93401
TELEPHONE: *(805) 545-9802; (800) 488-2045*
E-MAIL: *innkeeper@gardenstreetinn.com*
WEBSITE: *www.gardenstreetinn.com*
ROOMS: *9 Rooms; 4 Suites; All with private baths*
CHILDREN: *Children over the age of 16 are welcome*
ANIMALS: *Prohibited*

call first

Santa Clara Quiche

Makes 12 servings.

An easy do-ahead recipe. Prepare the batter for this quiche in advance, and refrigerate it 8 to 10 hours. When you're ready to cook, it's ready to bake.

4 tablespoons butter
10 eggs
¼ cup all-purpose flour
1 teaspoon baking powder
2 (14-ounce) cans artichoke hearts, drained and chopped
3 cups small-curd cottage cheese
3 cups shredded Monterey Jack cheese
1 teaspoon hot pepper sauce (such as Tabasco)

Melt the butter in a 13x9-inch glass baking dish; tilt to coat the sides and bottom. In a large bowl, mix together the eggs, flour, and baking powder. Add the melted butter remaining in the baking dish to the egg/flour mixture. Stir in the chopped artichoke hearts, cottage cheese, Monterey Jack cheese, and hot pepper sauce. Pour the batter into the prepared baking dish. Cover, and refrigerate 8 to 10 hours. When ready to cook, preheat the oven to 325°F. Bake for about 50 minutes, or until the edges begin to brown. Cool on a wire rack for 5 minutes, and then cut into serving pieces.

Sonoma Green Chile Eggs

Makes 10 to 12 portions.

1 pound ground breakfast
  sausage
½ cup all-purpose flour
½ cup yellow cornmeal
10 to 12 canned whole green
  chiles, rinsed of seeds and
  drained (the label will tell
  you how many whole chiles
  are in the can)
10 to 12 sticks Sonoma Jack or
  Monterey Jack cheese, cut
  about 3 inches long x ¼- to
  ½-inch wide to fit chiles
12 eggs

1 cup small-curd cottage cheese
½ cup canned evaporated milk
1 teaspoon baking powder
¼ cup (½ stick) butter, melted
  and cooled
Salt and pepper
1 cup grated Cheddar cheese
½ cup diced onion
½ cup fresh or frozen corn
  (optional)
Three-Pepper Sauce (recipe on
  page 148)
Chopped cilantro, for garnish

Preheat the oven to 350°F. Coat a 13x9-inch baking dish with nonstick cooking spray. In a medium skillet, brown the sausage; drain. Distribute the cooked sausage evenly on the bottom of the prepared baking dish. On a flat plate, mix the flour and cornmeal together. Stuff each chile with 1 stick cheese, and roll in the flour/cornmeal mixture. (Discard any leftover flour mixture.) Place the stuffed chiles in two rows over the cooked sausage. In a large mixing bowl, beat together the eggs, cottage cheese, evaporated milk, baking powder, melted butter, and salt and pepper to taste. Pour the egg mixture over the top of the chiles and sausage. Sprinkle the Cheddar cheese, diced onion, and corn, if using, on top. Bake for 45 to 50 minutes, or until firm and no longer liquid in the center. Cut into pieces; top each serving with the Three-Pepper Sauce and garnish with the cilantro.

Make-ahead tip: This dish may be assembled the night before serving. Cover and refrigerate; bake the next day.

(For inn information see page 102)

Fresh Vegetable Frittata

Makes 10 servings.

2 to 3 tablespoons olive oil
1 large red onion, sliced
3 cloves garlic, sliced
3 yellow squash, sliced ¼-inch thick
3 zucchini, sliced ¼-inch thick
1 red bell pepper, sliced into thin strips
1 yellow bell pepper, sliced into thin strips
1 green bell pepper, sliced into thin strips
8 ounces fresh mushrooms, sliced
8 large eggs
¼ cup milk, half-and-half, or cream

6 to 8 tiny red potatoes, steamed and sliced
2 teaspoons salt
2 teaspoons freshly ground black pepper
1 teaspoon dried basil (or use ¼ cup slivered fresh basil leaves)
2 cups French bread cubes (½-inch pieces)
1 (8-ounce) package cream cheese, cut into small cubes
2 cups grated Swiss or mozzarella cheese
½ cup grated Parmesan cheese

In a very large sauté pan, heat the olive oil, and sauté the red onion and garlic for a minute or two. Add the squash, zucchini, peppers, and mushrooms; sauté until the vegetables are just barely tender. Do not over-cook. Let the mixture cool. In a very large bowl, beat the eggs with the milk. Add the potatoes, salt, pepper, basil, bread cubes, cream cheese, Swiss cheese, Parmesan cheese, and the cooled vegetable mixture. Fold the ingredients together gently but thoroughly. Preheat the oven to 350°F. Pack the mixture into a lightly greased 10x2-inch springform pan. Place the pan on a rimmed cookie sheet (to catch any drips). Bake 1 hour, or until the center is set. Let the frittata cool for 10 minutes, unmold, slice, and serve.

Serving suggestion: In the spring and summer, garnish the frittata with a dollop of sour cream, fresh tomato slices, and a sprig of fresh basil. In the fall and winter, the frittata is delicious served with a hollandaise sauce.

(For inn information see page 98)

Wine Country Inn

T he Wine Country Inn is a welcome retreat for weary travelers, wine
lovers, and those who seek a peaceful haven. Perched on a knoll
overlooking manicured vineyards, this captivating inn offers individually
decorated guest rooms. Fashioned after classic New England inns, all
guest rooms are individually decorated with antiques, family made quilts,
fireplaces, and balconies.

The Napa Valley is blessed with six very distinct seasons. The most
popular is the harvest season that runs from mid-August to mid-October.
Large gondolas (grape trailers) rumble down the highways, literally turning
the roads black with dripping juice.

INNKEEPER:	*Jim Smith*
ADDRESS:	*1152 Lodi Lane*
	St. Helena, CA 94574
TELEPHONE:	*(707) 963-7077*
E-MAIL:	*romance@winecountryinn.com*
WEBSITE:	*www.winecountryinn.com*
ROOMS:	*20 Rooms; 4 Suites; All with private baths*
CHILDREN:	*Discouraged*
ANIMALS:	*Prohibited*

designated areas   call first   call first

Sourdough Egg Casserole

Makes 8 to 12 servings.

Although this breakfast/brunch dish is not difficult to make, it does require some advance planning. Start the recipe the day or night before, since the bread mixture must sit in the refrigerator 8 to 10 hours to soak up the liquid.

12 slices extra-sourdough bread
Butter, room temperature
2 plus 2 cups grated Cheddar cheese
½ medium onion, diced
1 cup thinly sliced mushrooms
10 eggs
4 cups milk
3 heaping tablespoons spicy mustard (such as Dijon)
1 teaspoon salt
¼ teaspoon pepper

Coat a 13x9-inch baking dish with a nonstick spray. Lightly butter the bread slices. Cut the slices into small cubes; place half the bread cubes in the baking dish. Sprinkle with 2 cups of the cheese, diced onion, and mushroom slices. Add a second layer of bread, and top with the remaining 2 cups cheese. In a large bowl, beat together the eggs, milk, mustard, salt, and pepper. Pour this mixture evenly over the bread mixture. Refrigerate, covered, 8 to 10 hours. When ready to cook, preheat the oven to 325°F. Bake, uncovered, for 50 to 60 minutes (or longer if necessary) until the top is golden and lightly crusted. Let the casserole sit for 10 to 15 minutes before serving.

South of the Border
Crustless Quiche

Makes 8 to 12 servings.

1 loaf white or whole-wheat French bread, cut into 1-inch cubes
1 (7-ounce) can diced green chiles
8 to 12 ounces (2–3 cups) shredded Monterey Jack cheese
8 to 12 ounces (2–3 cups) shredded Cheddar cheese
6 ounces feta cheese with basil and tomato
9 eggs
1½ to 2 cups milk
Salt and pepper
Salsa, for serving (homemade or purchased)

Preheat the oven to 350°F. Coat a 13x9-inch glass baking dish with nonstick cooking spray. Place the bread cubes on the bottom of the prepared baking dish. In a large bowl, mix the chiles with the three cheeses. Sprinkle the chile/cheese mixture over the bread cubes. Using the same bowl, beat together the eggs and milk. Season with salt and pepper to taste. Pour the egg/milk mixture over all the ingredients in the baking dish. Bake for 45 minutes, or until a toothpick inserted near the center comes out clean. Let the quiche stand for 5 to 10 minutes before cutting into serving pieces. Serve with salsa.

(For inn information see page 34)

Spinach Quiche

Makes 9 to 12 servings.

Complement this crustless breakfast quiche with hot muffins, browned sausage links, and colorful fresh fruit—a very satisfying combo.

4 tablespoons butter
1 package (10 ounces) washed, ready-to-eat fresh baby spinach or 2
**   bunches fresh spinach, washed and coarsely chopped**
Salt (about ½ teaspoon)
Fresh garlic (about 2 cloves, minced)
10 eggs, beaten
3 cups (24 ounces) small- or large-curd cottage cheese
1 cup (4 ounces) shredded Monterey Jack cheese
¼ cup dry bread crumbs (homemade or purchased Italian style)
Sour cream, for garnish (optional)

Preheat the oven to 350°F. Grease a 13x9-inch baking dish. In a large sauté pan, melt the butter. Add the spinach and the salt and garlic to taste. Cook until the spinach is wilted and tender, about 7 to 10 minutes. Drain in a colander and cool. In a large bowl, mix together the beaten eggs, cottage cheese, Monterey Jack cheese, and the bread crumbs. Squeeze any remaining moisture from the cooled spinach and add to the egg/cheese mixture. Mix well, and pour into the prepared baking dish. Bake for 35 to 45 minutes, or until lightly browned and a knife inserted near the center of the quiche comes out clean. Let the quiche stand for 5 to 10 minutes before cutting into serving pieces. If desired, garnish each piece with a dollop of the sour cream.

(For inn information see page 90)

Anderson Creek Boursin Cheese
Apricot Chutney
Curry Cheese Spread
Fruit Syrup
Green Tartar Sauce
Honey Butter
Mango Butter Sauce
Orange Syrup
Raspberry Syrup
Three-Pepper Sauce
Basil Hollandaise Sauce
Vanilla Sauce

Sauces, Syrups, & Spreads

Anderson Creek Inn

Nestled in an enchanting valley near Mendocino Creek, the Anderson Creek Inn tastefully blends the beauty of the Anderson Valley with old-fashioned hospitality. Views from this lovely ranch-style inn encompass California's rolling hills that are peppered with majestic oak trees and magnificent redwoods. While leisurely strolling through the inn's sixteen acres, guests can observe a variety of farm animals before investigating the tree house with its hammock built for two.

Each morning the aroma of homemade pastries entices guests to the dining room where a delicious breakfast awaits them. Appetizing hors d'oeuvres are served daily between five and six o'clock.

INNKEEPERS:	*Jim & Grace Minton*
ADDRESS:	*12050 Anderson Valley Way*
	Boonville, CA 95415
TELEPHONE:	*(707) 895-3091; (800) 552-6202*
E-MAIL:	*innkeeper@andersoncreekinn*
WEBSITE:	*www.andersoncreekinn.com*
ROOMS:	*5 Rooms; All with private baths*
CHILDREN:	*Unsuitable*
ANIMALS:	*Prohibited; Resident dogs*

designated areas

Anderson Creek Boursin Cheese

Makes approximately 2 cups.

Spread this delicious herb-flavored boursin (boor-SAHN) on crackers, and serve as an hors d'oeuvre.

½ cup (1 stick) unsalted butter, room temperature
2 (8-ounce) packages cream cheese, room temperature
3 cloves garlic, minced
½ teaspoon salt
1 teaspoon dried oregano
¼ teaspoon dried thyme
¼ teaspoon dried dill weed
¼ teaspoon dried marjoram
¼ teaspoon dried basil
¼ teaspoon white pepper

In a food processor, combine the butter and cream cheese until smooth. In a small bowl, make a paste of the minced garlic and salt. Add the garlic paste, herbs, and pepper to cheese mixture and process for approximately 30 seconds. Refrigerate for several hours, allowing flavors to blend.

Make-ahead tip: This cheese spread may be made a day or two in advance. Refrigerate until ready to serve.

Apricot Chutney

Makes 2½ cups.

Make entertaining easy: prepare this spicy condiment on a day when you have time. Keep refrigerated until ready to use. Delicious as an appetizer served with cream cheese on bread or crackers, or as an accompaniment to Indian curries.

1 tablespoon vegetable oil
1 large onion, chopped
1 tablespoon grated fresh ginger
1 tablespoon whole mustard seed
1 teaspoon curry powder
½ teaspoon cayenne pepper
2 cups coarsely chopped dried apricots
⅔ cup golden raisins
½ cup vinegar
⅓ cup sugar
Salt
⅓ cup chopped fresh cilantro

In a large, nonstick sauté pan, combine the oil, onion, and ginger. Over medium heat, cook until lightly browned. Add the mustard seed, curry powder, and cayenne pepper. Stir for 4 minutes. Add the apricots, raisins, vinegar, and sugar. Cook for 7 minutes. Taste a sample, and add salt if desired. Stir in the cilantro. Remove from the heat and let cool. Place the cooled chutney in a covered container, and refrigerate until ready to serve.

(For inn information see page 64)

Curry Cheese Spread

Makes 4 cups spread.

This great, make-ahead appetizer is a large recipe that can easily be cut in half, if desired. Remember to set out a cheese spreader or other small knife when serving.

16 ounces finely grated sharp Cheddar cheese
1 cup finely chopped walnuts
1 cup mayonnaise
¼ cup finely diced onion or green onion
½ teaspoon curry powder
Hot pepper sauce
Crackers of choice

In a large bowl, combine the cheese, walnuts, mayonnaise, onion, curry, and pepper sauce; mix well. Pack the cheese spread into a jar, crock, or serving bowl. Chill several hours until firm. Serve with an assortment of crackers.

"We had a truly wonderful weekend here. The food was delicious! The best breakfasts we've had at a B&B!"
—Guest, Arroyo Village Inn

(For inn information see page 90)

Fruit Syrup

Makes 3 to 4 servings.

½ **cup packed brown sugar**
½ **cup pure maple syrup**
¼ **cup (½ stick) butter**
½ **teaspoon cinnamon**
¼ **cup dried cranberries**
¼ **cup dried apricots, cut into fourths**

In a small saucepan, combine the brown sugar, maple syrup, butter, cinnamon, cranberries, and apricots. Bring to a simmer, and cook for about 5 minutes. Remove the pan from the heat and let the syrup sit for 20 to 30 minutes before serving.

Make-ahead tip: The syrup may be made up to a week in advance. Cool, cover, and refrigerate. Reheat before serving over French toast.

(For inn information see page 98)

Green Tartar Sauce

Makes about 1 cup sauce.

This is a special sauce to go with the Salmon Burgers (recipe on page 194). It's so tasty you'll enjoy trying it with other seafood as well.

¾ **cup mayonnaise**
¼ **cup coarsely chopped cornichon pickles (see Carol's Corner)**
3 tablespoons capers, drained
1 large shallot, coarsely chopped
1 teaspoon lemon juice
½ **teaspoon Dijon mustard**
3 tablespoons coarsely chopped fresh chives
3 tablespoons coarsely chopped fresh parsley
2 tablespoons coarsely chopped fresh dill
½ **teaspoon pepper**

In a food processor, combine the mayonnaise, pickles, capers, shallot, lemon juice, mustard, chives, parsley, dill, and pepper. Process the mixture until it reaches the desired consistency. Cover and refrigerate for at least 2 hours before serving to allow the flavors to blend.

Make-ahead tip: Tartar sauce may be made a day or two in advance. Cover, and store in the refrigerator until ready to serve.

Carol's Corner
Cornichon (KOR-nih-shohn) pickles are tiny, crisp, and tart. They are more expensive than most pickles but have a unique flavor. If you can't find them at your regular grocery store, try a specialty foods market. Dill pickles may be substituted in the above recipe if necessary.

(For inn information see page 54)

Honey Butter

Makes ¾ cup.

Serve this delicious Honey Butter with Lemon Poppy Seed Pancakes (recipe on page 67). The Honey Butter is also wonderful on hot baking powder biscuits or toasted English muffins.

½ cup (1 stick) butter, melted
½ cup honey

Using a whisk, add the honey slowly to the melted butter. Whisk until the mixture is smooth and opaque. Let the honey butter cool, whisking several times to keep the mixture incorporated. Serve at room temperature on pancakes, biscuits, or muffins. Store Honey Butter in the refrigerator.

(For inn information see page 66)

Mango Butter Sauce

Makes 12 to 14 servings.

The addition of this warm sauce makes a fresh fruit cup extra special. The sauce may be prepared in advance and refrigerated. Reheat briefly in the microwave, or on the stovetop before serving.

2 cups mango nectar
¼ cup sugar
1 cup (2 sticks) butter, room temperature
Fresh fruit of choice (use a colorful mixture), cut into bite-size
    pieces
Mint sprigs, for garnish

In a large saucepan over medium heat, combine the mango nectar with the sugar. Bring to a simmer, and cook, stirring occasionally, until the mixture is reduced to 1 cup. Remove the pan from the heat, and slowly whisk in the softened butter until smooth. Keep slightly warm. Spoon the fruit into individual serving dishes. Pour a small amount of sauce over the fruit. Garnish each dish with a sprig of mint.

Note: You may substitute mango juice or passion fruit juice if mango nectar is not available, but the nectar is preferred. Look for the nectar in the supermarket in the canned fruit juice department.

(For inn information see page 112)

Orange Syrup

Makes 3 cups syrup.

3 tablespoons cornstarch
⅔ cup sugar
2 cups orange juice
½ cup butter, melted
2 tablespoons grated orange peel (zest)
Maple syrup (about ½ cup)

In a medium saucepan, combine the cornstarch and sugar. Gradually stir in the orange juice until smooth. Add the melted butter. Bring to a boil, continually stirring with a whisk (mixture will thicken). Lower the heat, and simmer for 5 minutes. Remove from the heat, add the grated orange peel, and add the maple syrup to desired taste and consistency.

Make-ahead tip: For convenience, the syrup can be prepared in advance. Just reheat when ready to use.

(For inn information see page 72)

Raspberry Syrup

Makes about 2 cups.

Try this delicious homemade syrup on the Lemon Soufflé Pancakes on page 69.

1½ cups light corn syrup
1½ cups fresh red raspberries
2 tablespoons lemon juice

In a large saucepan, combine the corn syrup and raspberries. Bring to a boil; lower the heat, and simmer for 5 minutes. Remove from the heat, and allow to cool. Add the lemon juice and stir. Strain the mixture through a fine mesh strainer, pushing hard with the back of a spoon to remove the seeds. Discard the seeds. Syrup is ready to serve.

Make-ahead tip: This syrup may be made in advance. Keep refrigerated, in a covered container, until ready to use.

(For inn information see page 68)

Three-Pepper Sauce

Makes 2 to 3 cups.

Enjoy this flavorful sauce that takes pasta or egg dishes to new heights. Cavanagh Inn pairs this sauce with its Sonoma Green Chile Eggs (recipe on page 130).

¼ cup (½ stick) butter
¼ cup diced onions
1 red pepper, diced
1 yellow pepper, diced
1 orange pepper, diced
¼ teaspoon ground cumin
¼ teaspoon oregano
¼ teaspoon marjoram
Juice of 1 lemon, about 2 to 3 tablespoons
1 cup chicken stock
½ cup heavy cream
Salt and pepper

In a large skillet, melt the butter and sauté the onions over medium heat until just translucent. Add the red, yellow, and orange peppers and the cumin, oregano, and marjoram. Cook until peppers are tender. Add the lemon juice and chicken stock. Continue cooking until the mixture is reduced and thickened. Spoon 1 cup of the cooked mixture into a blender and mix on medium speed until puréed. Pour the purée into a large bowl and continue to purée the rest of the cooked mixture in the same manner until all has been blended. Pour all of the puréed mixture back into the skillet, whisk in the cream, and add salt and pepper to taste. Continue to cook until the sauce is thickened to desired consistency. Serve over eggs or pasta.

Make-ahead tip: The sauce may be made a day in advance and refrigerated. When ready to serve, reheat on medium-low heat, or in the microwave oven until hot.

(For inn information see page 102)

Basil Hollandaise Sauce

Makes about 1 cup.

This sauce is great when served warm over any poached egg dish, omelet or frittata.

½ **cup (1 stick) unsalted butter**
2 large egg yolks
4 teaspoons fresh lemon juice
2 teaspoons Dijon-style mustard
1 cup packed basil leaves
Salt and pepper

In a small pan, melt the butter over moderate heat; keep it warm. In a blender or food processor, blend the egg yolks, lemon juice, mustard, and basil leaves for 5 seconds. With the motor running, add the warm melted butter in a stream. Season with salt and pepper to taste. Store any leftover Hollandaise sauce in the refrigerator.

(For inn information see page 160)

Oak Knoll Inn

Like visiting a private retreat, guests of the Oak Knoll Inn indulge in relaxation and pampering. Surrounded by six hundred acres of Chardonnay vines with the Stage Leap Mountain as a backdrop and nestled behind a wall of cypress trees, this secluded inn occupies one of the most spectacular locations in Napa Valley.

The innkeepers provide a full-time concierge service. One specialized itinerary consists of visiting small, exclusive wineries where guests are invited to participate in wine blending.

Breakfast is a feast at the Oak Knoll Inn. This scrumptious bounty is served each morning outside on the sunny deck or by the crackling fireplace on nippy winter mornings. In the early evening, guests enjoy a wine and cheese party, often with a visiting wine maker.

INNKEEPER:	*Barbara Passino*
ADDRESS:	*2200 E. Oak Knoll Avenue*
	Napa Valley, CA 94558
TELEPHONE:	*(707) 255-2200*
E-MAIL:	*Not available*
WEBSITE:	*www.oakknollinn.com*
ROOMS:	*4 Rooms; All with private baths*
CHILDREN:	*Children over the age of 14 are welcome*
ANIMALS:	*Prohibited*

designated areas

Vanilla Sauce

Makes 8 servings.

Serve this delicious, delicate sauce with Stuffed Baked Pears (recipe on page 231). The sauce is also a perfect accompaniment to dessert soufflés, bread puddings, or other hot desserts.

2 cups half-and-half
2 teaspoons vanilla extract (or use a vanilla bean)
1 teaspoon brandy
2 plus 2 tablespoons sugar
2 egg yolks

In a medium saucepan, combine the half-and-half, vanilla, brandy, and 2 tablespoons sugar. Heat almost to a simmer. In a small bowl, whisk the egg yolks and the remaining 2 tablespoons of sugar together. Whisk a tablespoon of the warmed half-and-half mixture into the egg yolk mixture; then add another tablespoon and another, whisking continually. Once the egg yolk mixture is warm and smooth, pour it into the remaining half-and-half mixture. Over low heat, whisk until the sauce is thickened slightly. Remove from the heat, cool, and store in the refrigerator. Serve chilled.

Make-ahead tip: Vanilla Sauce may be made a day in advance.

Chilled Cucumber-Raisin-Walnut Soup

Corn Chowder

Elk Cove Inn Clam Chowder

Fruit Soup

Jicama-Corn-Tomato Salad

Mrs. B's Spinach Salad

Lightly Curried Cauliflower Soup

Waldorf Salad with Sweet & Spicy Candied Pecans

Soups
&
Salads

Chilled Cucumber-Raisin-Walnut Soup

Makes 6 cups (about 8 servings as a first course).

This tart and tangy soup, sweetened with raisins, makes a cool and refreshing starter for a summer dinner party. And the bonus—it's incredibly easy. Make the soup in advance, and serve it well chilled.

1 cup raisins
3 to 4 cucumbers, peeled and seeded
5 green onion tops
¾ cup walnuts
2 cups heavy cream
2 cups plain yogurt
Salt and pepper
Chopped green onions, for garnish
Chopped walnuts, for garnish
Thin cucumber slices, unpeeled, for garnish

Soak the raisins in 2 cups warm water for about 20 minutes until they are plump; drain. In a food processor, finely chop the cucumbers. Place in a large bowl. Repeat the process with the green onion tops and then the walnuts. Stir in the cream and the yogurt. Add the drained raisins. Season with salt and pepper to taste. Chill several hours before serving. To serve, ladle the soup into individual bowls; place a small amount of garnish in the center.

(For inn information see page 36)

Corn Chowder

Makes 6 to 8 servings.

4 medium potatoes, cut into small cubes
4 slices bacon
2 plus 4 tablespoons butter
4 medium mild onions, cut into slices and then cut in half
1 quart (4 cups) whole milk
½ cup light cream
2 (15¼-ounce) cans cream-style corn
½ cup potato water
¼ teaspoon dried parsley flakes
¼ teaspoon thyme
¼ teaspoon marjoram
1½ teaspoons salt
½ teaspoon pepper
Paprika and fresh parsley, for garnish

In a large saucepan, cook the cubed potatoes in simmering water for 15 minutes. Drain the potatoes, reserving ½ cup of the potato water. In a large sauté pan, fry the bacon slices. Remove the bacon and crumble; pour off the fat, but do not wash the pan. Add the 2 tablespoons butter to the pan, and sauté the onions until brown. In a large soup pot, warm the milk and cream. Add the cooked potatoes, browned onions, bacon, and canned corn. Using the reserved potato water, rinse the empty corn cans and add the liquid to the soup pot. Add the remaining 4 tablespoons butter, parsley flakes, thyme, marjoram, salt, and pepper. Heat the soup to a simmer before serving. Ladle the soup into individual serving bowls. Garnish each serving with a sprinkling of paprika and a small parsley sprig.

(For inn information see page 72)

Elk Cove Inn
Clam Chowder

Makes 8 servings.

10 ounces hickory-smoked bacon, diced
4 medium yellow onions, diced
1 tablespoon minced garlic
2 carrots, diced
8 ribs celery, diced
1 tablespoon fresh chopped thyme, or ½ teaspoon dried
½ teaspoon salt
¼ teaspoon ground pepper
1 cup dry white wine
4 large russet potatoes, peeled and diced
1 (3-pound) can chopped ocean clams, drained (save juice)
½ cup flour
½ teaspoon hot sauce
1 tablespoon Worcestershire sauce
¾ cup heavy cream (or more)

In a stockpot, cook the bacon. Add the onions and garlic to bacon, and sauté until clear. Add the carrots, celery, thyme, salt, and pepper, and sauté another 5 minutes. Pour in the wine, reduce until syrupy, and add the potatoes. Sauté another 10 minutes. Add the drained clam juice, and cook until the potatoes and vegetables are done. Add the flour, hot sauce, and Worcestershire sauce, and cook until the flour is dissolved. Add the clams and cream to desired consistency, and heat until hot.

(For inn information see page 54)

Fruit Soup

Makes about 8 servings.

Stock:
1 cup cranberry juice
1 cup apple juice
½ cup orange juice
½ cup watermelon, seeded and puréed
½ cup strawberries, stems removed and puréed
½ cup peaches, pitted and puréed
1 cup banana, puréed
⅓ cup fresh lemon or lime juice
Fresh mint leaves, blended in with fruit, optional
¼ teaspoon cardamom, optional
¼ teaspoon cinnamon, optional
¼ cup red wine, optional
¼ cup champagne or white sauterne, optional

Fruit:
½ cup strawberries, stems removed and sliced
½ cup watermelon, seeded and cut bite-size
½ cup seedless grapes, cut in half
½ cup peaches and/or nectarines, peeled, pitted, and sliced
½ cup pineapple chunks
½ cup cantaloupe balls
½ cup honeydew balls
Any other fruit of the season
Whipped cream, for garnish
Vanilla yogurt, for garnish
Sour cream, for garnish
Fresh mint sprigs, for garnish

In a large bowl, combine the cranberry juice, apple juice, orange juice, watermelon, strawberries, peaches, banana, lemon or lime juice, and any optional ingredients for the liquid base of the soup.

In another large bowl, combine the strawberries, watermelon, grapes, peaches, pineapple, cantaloupe, and honeydew. To serve, portion the fruit evenly into the individual serving bowls. Ladle the stock over the fruit. Garnish with a dollop of the whipped cream, vanilla yogurt, or sour cream. Top with a fresh mint sprig.

Make-ahead tip: The stock may be made a day ahead of time, and the flavor actually improves as the stock stands. Cover, and refrigerate.

(For inn information see page 64)

Jicama-Corn-Tomato Salad

Makes 8 to 12 servings.

A very refreshing and unique salad—just right for a summer day.

1 large jicama, cut into ½-inch cubes
3 ears fresh corn, boiled for 3 minutes, cut off cob
3 firm, ripe, fresh tomatoes, seeded and chopped
2 jalapeño peppers (or more, if desired), seeded and diced
½ to ¾ cup onion, chopped
1 cup chopped fresh cilantro
½ cup olive oil
¼ cup seasoned rice vinegar
Salt and pepper

In a large bowl, combine the jicama, corn, tomatoes, peppers, onion, cilantro, oil, and vinegar, tossing until fully mixed. Season with salt and pepper to taste. Chill for at least 2 hours before serving.

Note: When cooking the ears of corn, after the 3 minutes are up, plunge the corn into very cold water to stop the cooking process. This will help preserve the sweetness and fresh corn flavor.

Carol's Corner
A jicama (HEE-kah-mah) is often referred to as the Mexican potato. It is a large, bulbous root vegetable with a fibrous, brown skin that must be cut away before using. The flesh is white, crisp, and juicy and has the texture and taste similar to a cross between an apple and a radish (without the hotness). Jicama can be eaten raw or cooked. I especially enjoy it raw as a healthy snack cut into sticks.

(For inn information see page 66)

Mrs. B's Spinach Salad

Makes 6 to 8 servings.

Dressing:
4 teaspoons sugar
1 teaspoon dry mustard
⅓ cup cider vinegar
1 cup mild olive oil

Salad:
1 (1-pound) bag fresh baby spinach leaves, stems removed
1 head red leaf lettuce, torn into bite-size pieces
½ pound bacon, cooked, drained, and crumbled into small pieces
3 hard-cooked eggs, chopped
1 small red onion, sliced
4 ounces feta cheese, crumbled
Salt and pepper

In a small bowl, whisk together the sugar, dry mustard, vinegar, and oil; mix well. In a large bowl, combine the spinach, lettuce, bacon, eggs, onion, and feta cheese. Add the dressing to the toss salad. Season with the salt and pepper and serve.

(For inn information see page 126)

$\mathcal{A}$pplewood Inn

E ncircled by apple orchards and towering redwoods, the Applewood Inn is the perfect setting for a romantic bed and breakfast getaway or an idyllic wine country honeymoon. Relaxed and romantic accommodations are standard features of the Russian River Valley's Applewood Inn. Luxurious amenities include bedside fireplaces, Egyptian cotton towels, fine hand-pressed linens and European down pillows and comforters. All suites are air-conditioned.

The Applewood Inn Restaurant offers Sonoma dining at its best. Tuesday through Saturday evenings, in the distinguished Applewood Inn Restaurant, guests and visitors dine on the ever-changing delicious cuisine that focuses on fresh, impeccably prepared regional fare.

INNKEEPERS:	*Jim Caron & Darryl Notter*
ADDRESS:	*13555 Highway 116*
	Guerneville, CA 95446
TELEPHONE:	*(707) 869-9093; (800) 555-8509*
E-MAIL:	*stay@applewoodinn.com*
WEBSITE:	*www.applewoodinn.com*
ROOMS:	*9 Rooms; 7 Suites; All with private baths*
CHILDREN:	*Unsuitable*
ANIMALS:	*Prohibited*

Lightly Curried Cauliflower Soup

Makes 6 servings as a first course.

Chef Brian Gerritsen at the Applewood Inn and Restaurant suggests using a high-quality Madras curry powder for this recipe. He cautions, "Be sure to cook the spices for at least 5 minutes to ensure that the true essence of the spice blend is released."

**2 tablespoons butter
1 medium yellow onion, peeled and diced small
1 tablespoon plus a pinch of salt
1 teaspoon Madras curry powder (Madras is hotter than standard)
1 head cauliflower, trimmed and cut into 1-inch pieces
4 cups water
¼ cup heavy cream
2 or 3 very thin slices prosciutto, divided into 6 small pieces and
    rolled up for garnish**

In a heavy-bottom stockpot, melt the butter over medium heat. Add the onions with a pinch of salt, and cook until the onions are soft and translucent, about 10 minutes. Take care not to allow the onions to brown. Add the curry powder; stir, and cook at least 5 minutes. Add the cauliflower to the pot along with the water, cream, and the 1 tablespoon salt. Bring to a simmer, and cook over medium heat for about 25 minutes, until the cauliflower is tender. In a blender, purée the soup until smooth. Taste, and adjust the seasoning if necessary. To serve, ladle the soup into bowls; garnish each serving with the prosciutto.

Note: Prosciutto, a seasoned, Italian, salt-cured ham, is available in the deli section of most supermarkets and in gourmet and Italian markets.

Country Inn

S urrounded by graceful chandeliers, magnificent art, redwood moldings, and fireplaces, guests of the Country Inn bed and breakfast delight in this cozy inn with its quiet charm. This beautifully renovated 1890s residence exudes a carefree turn-of-the-century ambiance that includes authentic replica brass and iron beds covered with elegant fluffy comforters and pillows.

Art museums, galleries, antique shops, dining, and Glass Beach are within walking distance. A short drive leads to a Noyo fishing village, party boats, coastal cruises, and state parks. Guests also enjoy local celebrations, including Paul Bunyan Days, the Whale Festival, and the world's largest salmon barbecue.

A bounteous breakfast buffet features fruit, muffins, nut and fruit breads, and freshly brewed coffee.

INNKEEPERS:	*Bruce & Cynthia Knauss*
ADDRESS:	*632 North Main Street*
	Fort Bragg, CA 95437
TELEPHONE:	*(707) 964-3737; (800) 831-5327*
E-MAIL:	*info@beourguests.com*
WEBSITE:	*www.beourguests.com*
ROOMS:	*8 Rooms; All with private baths*
CHILDREN:	*Welcome*
ANIMALS:	*Prohibited*

designated areas

Waldorf Salad with Sweet & Spicy Candied Pecans

Makes 12 servings.

Make entertaining easier: prepare the Sweet & Spicy Candied Pecans ahead of time (recipe on page 232), and they'll be ready to go when you serve this special salad.

⅔ **cup dried tart cherries**
1 cup boiling water
½ **cup mayonnaise**
3 tablespoons sour cream
2 tablespoons fresh lemon juice
1 teaspoon sugar
4 Granny Smith apples, unpeeled, cored, cut into ½-inch cubes
1⅓ **cups very thinly sliced celery (about 3 large ribs)**
1⅓ **cups red seedless grapes, halved**
Salt and pepper
Romaine lettuce leaves, washed and dried
Sweet & Spicy Candied Pecans (recipe on page 232)

Soak the dried cherries in the boiling water until softened, about 10 minutes, and drain. In a large bowl, whisk together the mayonnaise, sour cream, lemon juice, and sugar. Add the chopped apples, celery slices, grape halves, and drained cherries. Season with salt and pepper to taste. Chill before serving. To serve, arrange the lettuce on a large serving platter or on individual salad plates. Spoon the Waldorf Salad over the lettuce. Top with the Sweet & Spicy Candied Pecans.

Caramel Peanut Butter Apple Dip

Creamy Baked Breakfast Potatoes

Doris' Provolone & Pesto Layered Cheese Torte

Hot Artichoke Dip

Jim's Garlic Clam Dip

Olive Cheese Ball

Peppered Oysters

Saffron & Wild Mushroom Risotto

Pygmalion Party Plum Meatballs

Sausage Pinwheels

Savory Artichoke Dip

Sesame-Seared Sea Scallops with Aïoli

Shrimp Fantasies

Southern Spoon Bread (Corn Pudding)

Toasted Clam Rolls

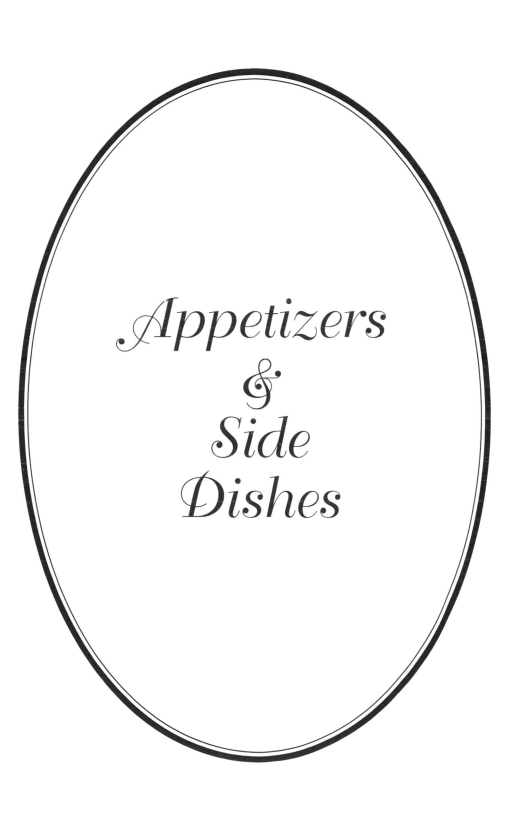

Appetizers
&
Side
Dishes

Jabberwock

The Jabberwock

O nce a convent, the Jabberwock is now a captivating bed and breakfast inn. Located directly above Cannery Row and the Monterey Bay Aquarium, the inn transports its guests through the looking glass into a wonderland of goose down pillows and comforters, Victorian beds with lace-trimmed sheets, and fresh flowers in every room. They also delight in the beauty of Monterey's coastline and relish in the unique attention and homemade goodies of this special inn.

A tantalizing breakfast is served by the fireplace in the dining room or in the privacy of each room. Early evening, a ringing bell beckons guests to the enclosed sun porch for hors d'oeuvres and beverages.

INNKEEPERS:	*Joan & John Kiliany; Johanna & Kip Richardson*
ADDRESS:	*598 Laine Street*
	Monterey, CA 93940
TELEPHONE:	*(831) 372-4777; (888) 428-7253*
E-MAIL:	*innkeeper@jabberwockinn.com*
WEBSITE:	*www.jabberwockinn.com*
ROOMS:	*5 Rooms; 1 Suite; Private baths in rooms; (Two rooms comprise suite, shared bath and sitting area)*
CHILDREN:	*Children over the age of 12 are welcome*
ANIMALS:	*Prohibited*

designated areas

Caramel Peanut Butter Apple Dip

Makes about 4 cups.

This dip is also great with banana chunks. Try it on graham crackers, too. No matter how you serve it, it's a welcome hors d'oeuvre or snack.

2 (8-ounce) packages cream cheese, room temperature
¾ cup packed brown sugar
½ cup peanut butter
½ cup sour cream
2 tablespoons vanilla
Apple slices
Lemon juice (optional)

In a medium bowl, using a mixer at low speed, combine the cream cheese, brown sugar, peanut butter, sour cream, and vanilla. Refrigerate until ready to use. Serve with the tart apple slices.

Note: To keep the apple slices from turning brown, toss them briefly in lemon juice, and then drain.

Carol's Corner
Another way to keep apple slices from turning brown is to toss them for a few seconds in some water to which salt has been added. Exact measurements are not necessary, but approximately ¼ teaspoon salt to 1 cup water works well. Drain the slices on paper towels.

Creamy Baked
Breakfast Potatoes

Makes 8 to 10 servings.

Don't let the word creamy *in the name fool you. If you are looking for a low-sodium/low-fat recipe, this one's for you.*

3 pounds potatoes (about 7 to 8 medium), peeled, cubed, and cooked
1 tablespoon dried minced onion
¼ teaspoon black pepper
1 (10¾-ounce) can Campbell's Healthy Request Cream of Broccoli
   soup
1 pint (16 ounces) nonfat sour cream (Beazley House prefers
   Knudsen or Naturally Yours brands of sour cream)
1 cup (4 ounces) sharp low-fat Cheddar cheese, grated
1 cup (4 ounces) mozzarella cheese, grated
1 cup corn flakes (crushed to measure ½ cup) for topping

Preheat the oven to 350°F. Coat a 13x9-inch baking dish with a nonstick cooking spray. Cook the potatoes (see directions below). While the potatoes are cooking, combine the onion, pepper, soup, sour cream, and cheeses in a large bowl. Add the cooked, drained potatoes, and mix well. Pour the mixture into the prepared baking dish. Sprinkle the corn flakes on top. Bake for approximately 45 minutes or until hot and bubbly.

Quick-cook method for potatoes: Peel the potatoes, and cut into ½-inch cubes. In a large saucepan, bring approximately 2 cups water to a boil. Add the cut-up potatoes, and cover tightly. Simmer for 5 to 10 minutes. The potatoes test done when easily pierced with a knife (potatoes should be tender, yet still firm). Drain immediately.

(For inn information see page 16)

Doris' Provolone & Pesto Layered Cheese Torte

Makes 16 to 20 servings.

Mixture:
8 to 12 ounces provolone
cheese, thinly sliced
2 (8-ounce) packages cream
cheese, room temperature
½ cup butter (1 stick), room
temperature
2 teaspoons minced garlic

Layers:
½ to 1 cup pesto, drained of
excess oil
½ cup oil-packed, sun-dried
tomatoes, well drained and
chopped
¼ cup pine nuts
Baguettes or crackers
Grapes, if desired

Line an 8-inch square pan with plastic wrap, extending the ends of the wrap over the edges of the pan. Line the pan with the provolone cheese (reserve a few slices for another layer of the torte), overlapping the slices a bit and pressing the edges together slightly. The cheese should extend over the edges of the pan enough that it can help encase the finished torte layers. Using a food processor, mix together the cream cheese, butter, and garlic. Spread the ingredients in layers in the following order:

> one-third of the mixture, one-half of the pesto, layer of provo-
> lone, sun-dried tomatoes, pine nuts, one-third of the mixture, the
> remaining pesto, and the remaining mixture.

Fold the sides of the cheese over the mixture to encase it, using another slice in the middle, if needed. Fold the edges of plastic wrap over the finished cheese torte, covering tightly. Refrigerate for several hours or overnight. To serve, invert the mold onto a cutting board, remove the plastic wrap, and cut the torte diagonally into halves or fourths. Serve with the crackers or baguette slices. Red and green grapes make a good accompaniment.

Note: This torte may also be made in two smaller molds (use 5x3x2-inch loaf pans), using half of the ingredients in each mold.

(For inn information see page 94)

Hot Artichoke Dip

Makes about 6 servings.

1 (14-ounce) can artichoke hearts (in water), drained and chopped
½ cup mayonnaise
½ cup plus 2 tablespoons grated Parmesan cheese
½ teaspoon garlic salt
Crackers, for serving

Preheat oven to 350°F. Mix the artichoke hearts, mayonnaise, ½ cup Parmesan cheese, and garlic salt together in a bowl. Spoon the mixture into an ungreased 8-inch round, shallow baking dish. Sprinkle the top with the remaining 2 tablespoons cheese, and bake for 20 minutes, or until hot and bubbly. Serve with crackers.

Make-ahead tip: The dip may be prepared a day in advance. Cover and refrigerate until ready to use.

(For inn information see page 88)

Jim's Garlic Clam Dip

Makes about 3 cups.

Wake up your taste buds. Serve this irresistible dip with rippled potato chips or a raw vegetable platter. The dip is best if made at least 2 hours in advance.

1 (8-ounce) package cream cheese
1 cup mayonnaise
1 teaspoon Worcestershire sauce
1 teaspoon lemon juice
½ teaspoon salt
1 heaping tablespoon finely chopped garlic
2 (6½-ounce) cans minced clams, drained and rinsed

Blend the cream cheese, mayonnaise, Worcestershire sauce, lemon juice, salt, and garlic in a food processor until smooth. In a medium bowl, combine the blended mixture with the clams, stirring with a spoon. Chill before serving.

Make-ahead tip: The dip may be prepared a day in advance. Refrigerate until ready to serve.

Carol's Corner
While I was testing recipes for this book, I took Jim's Garlic Clam Dip to a Fourth of July party at Angela and John's house—our wonderful neighbors across the street. After John's first taste, he said, "This is my new favorite dip. It has a bite to it that will hook you for life." I also served this dip when my brother and sister-in-law, Tom and Kay, came for a visit. They couldn't have agreed more.

(For inn information see page 132)

Olive Cheese Ball

Makes 3 balls or 24 servings.

2 (8-ounce) packages cream cheese
4 ounces bleu cheese
4 tablespoons (½ stick) butter
2 (4½-ounce) cans chopped ripe black olives, drained
4 heaping tablespoons chopped Italian parsley (flat-leaf)
4 green onions, chopped, white and green parts
⅓ to ½ cup walnuts, finely chopped
Crackers or celery, for serving

Blend in a mixer the cream cheese, bleu cheese, and butter. Add the chopped olives, parsley, and onions. Place in the refrigerator for an hour, or until firm. Divide the mixture evenly into three parts. Roll each portion into a ball, and then roll the balls in the walnuts. Wrap each cheese ball in plastic wrap and chill. Serve with crackers or stuff in celery sticks.

(For inn information see page 78)

Peppered Oysters

Makes 4 servings as an appetizer.

A special hors d'oeuvre for all you fried oyster lovers.

16 fresh oysters, small size
2 tablespoons freshly cracked pepper
½ cup all-purpose flour
½ cup peanut oil
1 tablespoon minced fresh garlic
1 tablespoon minced fresh shallots
1 large tomato, diced small
¼ cup Pernod (pehr-NOH), or other licorice-flavored liqueur
¼ cup white wine
2 cups fresh spinach (firmly packed), washed and stemmed
2 tablespoons butter, cut into small cubes
⅛ cup fresh lemon juice
Salt and pepper
Lemon wedges, for garnish

Drain the oysters in a colander to remove the excess liquid. Sprinkle the oysters with cracked pepper, and roll each in flour until evenly coated. In a large, shallow sauté pan, heat the peanut oil on medium high until just smoking. Carefully add the oysters, and cook until golden brown on one side (about 2 minutes). Turn the oysters, and cook until brown on the other side. Place 4 oysters off-center on each of 4 warm plates. Pour out the excess oil, leaving a tablespoon or two in the pan. Add the garlic, shallots, and tomatoes, and cook on medium heat for about 1 minute, stirring frequently. Add the Pernod, white wine, and spinach. Remove from the heat. Add the butter and lemon juice; stir until the butter is melted and spinach just starts to wilt. Sprinkle with salt and pepper to taste. Place some of the spinach mixture in the center of each plate holding the oysters. Pour a little of the sauce around the oysters and some over the spinach. Garnish each serving with a lemon wedge.

(For inn information see page 174)

Albion River Inn

L ocated on ten se-
cluded acres of gardens with spectacular ocean bluff views, the Albion River Inn is an ideal oceanfront destination. Rooms are individually decorated and furnished with a casual elegance that includes wood-burning fireplaces, spacious decks, and breathtaking views. Its romantic cliff-top restaurant features sumptuous coastal cuisine and award-winning wines. It was acclaimed by *Bon Appetit* magazine as, ". . . one of the finest to grace the Golden State shore." The restaurant lawn terrace and surrounding gardens are a popular setting for wedding receptions and private parties.

This scenic inn is located six miles south of Mendocino and minutes from galleries, boutiques, state parks, and beaches.

INNKEEPERS:	*Debbie Desmond & Doug Hynes*
ADDRESS:	*3790 Highway 1 North*
	Albion, CA 95410
TELEPHONE:	*(707) 937-1919; (800) 479-7944*
E-MAIL:	*innkeepers@albionriverinn.com*
WEBSITE:	*www.albionriverinn.com*
ROOMS:	*20 Rooms; All with private baths*
CHILDREN:	*Welcome (Due to cliff-top location, parents must supervise children at all times)*
ANIMALS:	*Prohibited; Resident cat*

designated areas

Saffron & Wild Mushroom Risotto

Makes 4 servings.

This is Chef Stephen Smith's special risotto recipe at Albion River Inn. He serves it alongside his Honey-Cured Bacon-Wrapped Quail (recipe on page 192).

4 cups chicken stock, or lightly-salted water
1 pinch saffron (adds both flavor and color)
¼ cup olive oil
1 small yellow onion, diced
4 shiitake mushroom caps, quartered

4 oyster mushroom caps, quartered
1 cup Arborio rice (Italian short-grained risotto rice)
2 ounces Asiago cheese, grated
4 tablespoons (½ stick) butter
6 large fresh basil leaves, chopped
Salt and pepper

In a small saucepan, bring the chicken stock or water to a boil. Lower the heat, and add the saffron; simmer for 5 minutes. (Keep the liquid hot until ready to use.) In a large, thick-bottom pan, heat the olive oil until almost smoking. Add the onion and both types of mushrooms; sauté for 1 minute. Add the rice, and sauté 2 more minutes, stirring constantly. Reduce the heat to medium, and add 1 cup of the hot saffron stock or water. Cook until almost all the liquid is absorbed. Repeat 3 more times (adding about 1 cup more each time) until all the liquid is used. When the rice looks creamy and all the liquid has been absorbed, add the cheese, butter, and basil. Stir until all is incorporated. Season with salt and pepper to taste. Serve immediately.

Serving suggestion: If the risotto is being served with the Honey-Cured Bacon Wrapped Quail, place a mound of risotto in the middle of each of 4 warm plates. Place two birds on each plate (one on each side of the risotto), and pour the sauce from the quail recipe over the birds. Serve with steamed or sautéed vegetables, such as beets, snow peas, squash, or corn.

Pygmalion House

L ocated at the end of a quiet residential street, the Pygmalion House bed and breakfast inn is a beautifully restored Queen Anne Victorian cottage. Full of antiques from the collections of the famous Gypsy Rose Lee and Sausalito Mayor Sally Stanford, this inn is a short walk from the Railroad Square, popular for its restaurants and specialty shops. This gracious bed and breakfast is an excellent point of departure for day trips to Sonoma and Napa wineries, Bodega Bay, Russian River recreation area, Muir Woods and the north coast beaches. There is also fishing, golfing, and horseback and bicycle riding nearby.

INNKEEPER:	*Caroline Berry*
ADDRESS:	*331 Orange Street*
	Santa Rosa, CA 95401
TELEPHONE:	*(707) 526-3407*
E-MAIL:	*Not available*
WEBSITE:	*www.bedandbreakfast.com*
ROOMS:	*6 Rooms; 1 Suite; All with private baths*
CHILDREN:	*Children over the age of eight are welcome*
ANIMALS:	*Prohibited*

Pygmalion Party
Plum Meatballs

Makes about 100 meatballs.

Planning a party? Make these crowd-pleasing, plum-sauced meatballs ahead of time, and store them in the freezer. On company day, just thaw and reheat, and they're ready to go.

Meatballs:
1 pound ground pork sausage, regular or spicy
1 pound ground beef
2 eggs
½ cup shallots (or onions), finely chopped
2 tablespoons chopped parsley
2 teaspoons salt
2 cups Italian-flavored dry bread crumbs
2 tablespoons butter (or margarine)

Sauce:
1 cup Pygmalion House plum jam (or other plum jam)
½ cup barbecue sauce

To make the meatballs, in a large bowl, mix together the pork, beef, eggs, shallots, parsley, salt, and bread crumbs. Roll into small, bite-size meatballs (1-inch or less in diameter). In a skillet over medium heat, brown the meatballs in the butter. Place the browned meatballs in a baking dish. Preheat the oven to 350°F.

To make the sauce, in a small bowl, combine the plum jam and barbecue sauce; pour the mixture over the meatballs. Bake, uncovered, for about 30 minutes, or until meatballs are hot and thoroughly cooked. Serve the meatballs in a chafing dish with toothpicks.

Dolores Park Inn

Located near the historic Mission Dolores, the Dolores Park Inn is a two-story Italianate Victorian mansion. Originally built in 1874, this charming inn is within walking distance of streetcar and subway lines, international restaurants, trendy boutiques, antique shops and tennis courts. This stately inn features four units, including one suite with a large deck, sunny patio, and garden.

A full gourmet breakfast is served each morning. Afternoon coffee, tea, or wine is served on the patio or by the fireplace.

INNKEEPER:	*Mr. Bernie H. Vielwerth*
ADDRESS:	*3641 Seventeenth Street*
	San Francisco, CA 94114
TELEPHONE:	*(415) 621-0482; (415) 553-6060*
E-MAIL:	*Not Available*
WEBSITE:	*Not Available*
ROOMS:	*3 Rooms; 1 Suite; 1 Cottage; Private & shared baths*
CHILDREN:	*Children over the age of 14 are welcome*
ANIMALS:	*Prohibited; Resident dogs and birds*

Sausage Pinwheels

Makes 12 biscuits.

These pinwheel-shaped biscuits are easy to make and especially nice served with an egg dish and fruit. An enjoyable breakfast treat.

1 (8-ounce) tube refrigerated crescent rolls
½ pound (8 ounces) uncooked bulk pork sausage
2 tablespoons minced, fresh chives

Preheat the oven to 375°F. Unroll the crescent roll dough on a lightly floured surface; press the seams and perforations together. Roll the dough into a 14x10-inch rectangle. Spread the sausage to within one-half inch of the edges. Sprinkle with the chives. Carefully roll up the dough from a long side; cut into twelve slices. Lay the slices, 1 inch apart, on an ungreased 15x10x1-inch baking sheet. Bake for 12 to 16 minutes, or until pinwheels are golden brown.

Inn at Depot Hill

The Inn at Depot Hill is a stately, 1900s railroad depot that has been lovingly transformed into a sophisticated seaside inn. Located two blocks from a sandy beach in the Mediterranean-style village of Capitola-by-the-Sea, the inn was named one of the top ten inns in the country. Under the exacting eye of San Francisco interior designer Linda L. Floyd, each of the guest rooms has been painstakingly decorated to evoke a singular time, place, and state of mind. All rooms feature a gas fireplace, TV with VCR, stereo, telephone with data port, and private luxurious marbled bathroom. Carmel, Monterey, and San Jose are just a short drive away.

A sumptuous breakfast is served in the morning, wine and hors d'oeuvres in the afternoon, and dessert in the evening.

INNKEEPERS: *Suzie Lankes and Dan Floyd*
ADDRESS: *250 Monterey Avenue*
Capitola-by-the-Sea, CA 95010
TELEPHONE: *(800) 572-2632*
E-MAIL: *lodging@innatdepothill.com*
WEBSITE: *www.innatdepothill.com*
ROOMS: *6 Rooms; 6 Suites; All with private baths*
CHILDREN: *Unsuitable*
ANIMALS: *Prohibited*

designated areas

Savory Artichoke Dip

Makes about 8 servings as an appetizer.

This dip/spread is very popular with guests at The Inn at Depot Hill. Try this winner for your next party.

2 (6-ounce) jars marinated artichoke hearts, drained and chopped
4 green onions, chopped (white and green parts)
1 cup shredded Parmesan cheese
½ cup mayonnaise
1 cup shredded mozzarella or Monterey Jack cheese
3 cloves garlic, minced
1 tablespoon pesto, optional
1 thinly sliced baguette, or crackers of choice

Preheat the oven to 350°F. In a medium bowl, mix together the artichokes, onions, Parmesan, mayonnaise, mozzarella, garlic, and pesto, if using. Spoon the mixture into an ungreased, ovenproof shallow dish (8 inches in diameter). Bake for about 20 to 25 minutes, or until bubbly and lightly browned. Let rest a few minutes. Serve with the baguette slices or crackers.

Make-ahead tip: The mixture can be prepared in advance, covered, and refrigerated until ready to bake.

Carol's Corner
This is one of the best artichoke dips I have ever tasted. Using marinated artichokes really makes a difference. Laura and Al (my sister and brother-in-law) thought this appetizer was so good, they plan to take it to their next tennis potluck. Tip: If you are lucky enough to have any dip left over (but I doubt it), you'll find it just as delicious reheated in the microwave the next day. What a treat!

Sesame-Seared Sea Scallops with Aïoli

Makes 12 appetizers or 4 main course servings.

Aïoli (ay-OH-lee) is a highly seasoned, flavorful garlic sauce that is drizzled over the scallops at serving time. It would make a nice accompaniment to other seafood as well. For stress-free preparation, make the aïoli a day or two in advance, and store it in the refrigerator.

Aïoli:

2 tablespoons fresh ginger, minced
¼ cup seasoned rice wine vinegar
Juice of 2 limes, about 5 tablespoons
1 egg

1 cup olive oil
½ tablespoon chopped fresh cilantro
½ tablespoon chopped fresh mint
½ tablespoon minced garlic
Salt and pepper

In a small sauté pan, combine the ginger, vinegar, and lime juice. Cook until most of the liquid has evaporated, and cool. In a medium bowl, whisk the egg. Continue to whisk rapidly while slowly drizzling in the oil to make emulsification (binding the ingredients together). Add the cilantro, mint, garlic, and the ginger/vinegar cooled mixture. Season with salt and pepper to taste, and refrigerate.

Scallops:

12 large scallops
2 tablespoons sesame seeds

¼ cup peanut oil
Fresh lime slices, for garnish

Rinse the scallops, and pat with paper towels. Sprinkle the scallops with the sesame seeds on both sides. In a sauté pan, heat the peanut oil until just smoking. Sear scallops for 2 minutes on each side, until golden brown. Place the scallops on serving plates, and drizzle with the aïoli. Garnish with lime slices.

(For inn information see page 174)

Shrimp Fantasies

Makes 42 appetizers.

½ **pound tiny, shelled, cooked shrimp**
1 cup mayonnaise
1 cup (4 ounces) shredded Swiss cheese
⅓ **cup chopped scallions (green onions)**
1 tablespoon fresh lemon juice
1½ **teaspoons chopped fresh dill (or ½ teaspoon dried dill weed)**
Dash of cayenne pepper
42 slices petite, cocktail, rye bread

In a medium bowl, combine the shrimp, mayonnaise, cheese, scallions, lemon juice, dill, and cayenne pepper. Preheat oven to 450°F. Grease a baking sheet. Top each slice of bread with about 1 tablespoon of the shrimp mixture. Arrange the slices in a single layer on the prepared baking sheet. Bake until the shrimp mixture is golden brown and bubbly, about 8 to 10 minutes. Serve immediately.

Make-ahead tip: Mixture may be made a day in advance. Cover and refrigerate until ready to use.

(For inn information see page 74)

Southern Spoon Bread
(Corn Pudding)

Makes 8 servings.

This is a great side dish to serve with chicken or pork.

1 (15-ounce) can cream style corn
1 (15¼-ounce) can whole kernel corn, drained
½ cup (1 stick) butter, melted
1 egg, beaten
1 cup sour cream
1 (8½-ounce) box or package corn muffin mix

Preheat the oven to 350°F. Coat a two-quart round casserole dish with nonstick cooking spray. In a large bowl, combine the cream style corn, whole corn, butter, egg, sour cream, and muffin mix. Mix well. Pour the mixture into the prepared casserole dish. Bake, uncovered, for approximately 1 hour.

Make-ahead tip: Bread may be mixed a day in advance. Cover, and refrigerate until ready to bake.

(For inn information see page 54)

Toasted Clam Rolls

Makes about 14 to 16 rolls.

3 (6½-ounce) cans minced clams
⅓ cup thinly sliced onion
½ cup mayonnaise
1 teaspoon Worcestershire sauce
¾ teaspoon garlic powder
¼ to ½ teaspoon hot sauce
6 tablespoons Parmesan cheese
14 to 16 slices white bread (thin-sliced)
6 tablespoons butter, melted

Preheat the oven to 425°F. In a medium bowl, combine the clams, onion, mayonnaise, Worcestershire sauce, garlic powder, hot sauce, and Parmesan cheese. Cut the crusts off the bread slices. With a rolling pin, roll the slices of bread very thin. Spread about 1 tablespoon of the clam mixture on each bread slice, and roll up. On a greased baking sheet, arrange the rolls about 1-inch apart. Using a pastry brush, brush each roll with the melted butter. Bake for approximately 12 minutes, or until lightly browned.

(For inn information see page 132)

Chicken Divan in Ramekins
Chili Relleno Soufflé
Cioppino for Two
Honey-Cured Bacon-Wrapped Quail
Parmesan Chicken
Salmon Burgers
Vizcaya Mushroom Sauté over Fresh Pasta

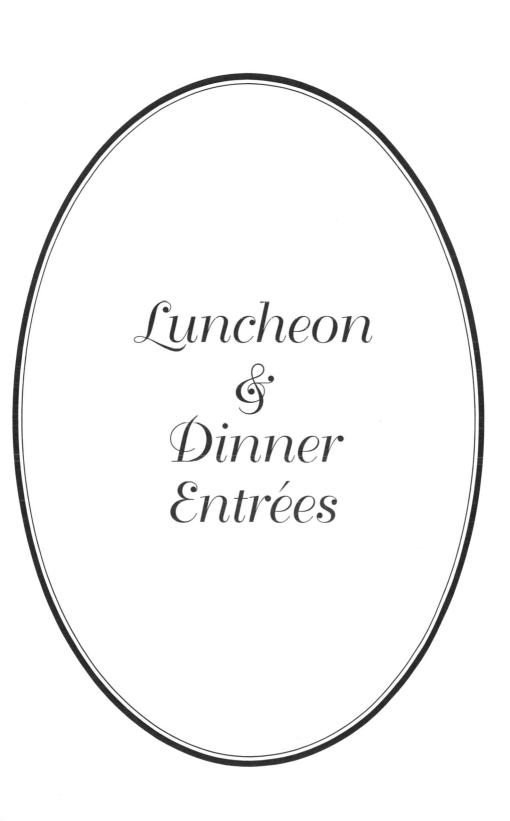

Luncheon
&
Dinner
Entrées

Chicken Divan in Ramekins

Makes 6 servings.

This recipe is easy to serve since it is baked in individual-sized portions. With a tossed lettuce salad and crusty French bread, this meal would be good for a luncheon or casual dinner.

10 to 14 ounces frozen chopped broccoli or broccoli florets
3 cups shredded cooked chicken (or turkey)
1 can (10¾ ounces) condensed cream of chicken soup
¼ cup mayonnaise
1 cup (4 ounces) shredded Cheddar cheese
Paprika, optional

Coat 6 individual ramekins (about 4 inches in diameter) with a nonstick cooking spray. Cook the broccoli according to the package directions (do not overcook); drain off any excess liquid. Divide the cooked broccoli evenly in the ramekins. Layer the cooked chicken over the broccoli. In a small bowl, combine the soup and mayonnaise; spread over the chicken. Sprinkle the cheese over the top. Preheat the oven to 350°F. Bake, uncovered, for 25 to 30 minutes, or until hot and set. If desired, before serving lightly sprinkle with the paprika for color.

Carol's Corner
A ramekin is an individual baking dish that resembles a miniature soufflé dish. Ramekins can be purchased in a variety of sizes and can be used for both baked and chilled dishes.

(For inn information see page 78)

Chili Relleno Soufflé

Makes 12 servings.

12 corn tortillas, cut into
 ¼-inch strips
1 tablespoon dried oregano
1 (16-ounce) can whole
 Anaheim chili peppers,
 seeded and sliced
2 large garlic cloves, finely
 diced
1 teaspoon lemon pepper
1 large onion, finely diced
1 teaspoon garlic salt
3 cups shredded cheese
 (combination of Cheddar/
 Monterey Jack)

1½ cups water
½ cup nonfat dry milk powder
1 teaspoon cayenne pepper
1 teaspoon ground coriander
1 teaspoon ground cumin
1 large tomato, cut into
 quarters
1 bunch fresh cilantro
1 cup all-purpose flour
8 large eggs
1 large red bell pepper, finely
 diced
Salsa, for topping
Sour cream, for topping

Grease a 13x9-inch baking dish. Cover the bottom of the dish with one-third of the tortilla strips. Sprinkle with the dried oregano. Layer with half the Anaheim chili slices. Sprinkle with diced garlic and lemon pepper. Cover with a second layer of tortilla strips. Layer the other one-half of Anaheim chili slices; sprinkle with the diced onion and garlic salt. Place the remaining tortilla strips on top, and cover with the shredded cheese. In a blender, combine the water, powdered milk, cayenne, coriander, cumin, tomato chunks, 10 cilantro sprigs, flour, and eggs. Mix for 2 minutes. Pour the egg mixture over the layers in the baking dish; top with the diced red pepper. Cover and refrigerate for at least 4 hours. Preheat the oven to 350°F, and then reduce the heat to 300°F. Bake for 45 minutes. Turn the temperature back up to 350°F, and bake 15 minutes longer, or until the center of the soufflé is set. Let cool 15 minutes before cutting. Serve with the salsa and sour cream; garnish with the cilantro sprigs.

(For inn information see page 28)

Auberge du Soleil

The exquisite French-accented country inn ambiance of the Auberge du Soleil (Inn of the Sun) echoes the Mediterranean feeling of California's wine country. All rooms and suites have private terraces and fireplaces.

For many, the name Auberge du Soleil connotes food first. The restaurant began in 1981, preceding the namesake by four years. The innovative menus complement the viticultural heritage of Napa Valley's bounty.

INNKEEPER:	*Philippa Perry, General Manager*
ADDRESS:	*180 Rutherford Hill Road*
	Rutherford, CA 94573
TELEPHONE:	*(707) 963-1211*
E-MAIL:	*reserve@aubergedusoleil.com*
WEBSITE:	*www.aubergedusoleil.com*
ROOMS:	*31 Rooms; 19 Suites; All with private baths*
CHILDREN:	*Unsuitable for children under the age of 16*
ANIMALS:	*Prohibited*

Cioppino for Two

Makes 2 servings.

Cioppino (chuh-PEE-noh) is a delicious fish stew that originated in San Francisco. The stew (actually more of a broth than a stew) is great ladled over rice or pasta and served with crusty French bread.

Broth:
2 tablespoons olive oil
2 tablespoons minced garlic
2 tablespoons minced shallots
3 tablespoons minced fennel
½ cup white wine
1 cup fish stock or bottled clam juice
1 cup chicken stock
1 cup canned tomato purée
1 bay leaf
1 teaspoon crushed red pepper (dried chili flakes)
1 tablespoon chopped parsley
1 tablespoon chopped chervil

Cioppino:
2 pieces (3 ounces each) of Chilean sea bass (or other firm mild white fish)
6 mussels
6 clams
3 ounces rock shrimp
2 large shrimp

To make the broth, heat the oil in a stockpot. Sauté the garlic, shallots, and fennel on medium heat until soft but not brown, about 3 to 5 minutes. Add the wine; cook until reduced by half. Add the fish stock or clam juice, chicken stock, tomato purée, bay leaf, crushed red pepper, parsley, and chervil. Simmer over low heat for 20 minutes.

To make the cioppino, in large sauté pan, cook the sea bass in a small amount of oil until golden on under side, about 3 minutes. Turn the fish over; add the mussels, clams, and both kinds of shrimp. Immediately add the hot broth. Cook until the clams and mussels open. Discard any that do not open. Serve in soup bowls.

Make-ahead tip: The broth may be made one day in advance and refrigerated. Reheat before using in the recipe.

Honey-Cured Bacon-Wrapped Quail

Makes 4 servings.

For a memorable meal, pair this with Saffron & Wild Mushroom Risotto (recipe on page 175).

Marinade:
2 tablespoons minced garlic
2 tablespoons minced shallots
2 tablespoons minced ginger
3 ounces soy sauce
3 ounces red wine vinegar
6 sprigs fresh thyme
1 tablespoon brown sugar
⅛ cup olive oil

Meat/Poultry:
8 slices honey-cured bacon
8 (4-ounce) quail, whole

Sauce:
Marinade
4 tablespoons butter

To make the marinade, in a small bowl, combine the garlic, shallots, ginger, soy sauce, vinegar, thyme, brown sugar, and oil, using a whisk. Wrap the bacon around the birds at the bottom of the breast, just above the legs. Fold the wings back, so the birds rest level. Place the birds breast down in a shallow pan, and pour the marinade mixture over them. Marinate for at least 8 hours, or overnight at the longest. Preheat the oven to 425°F. Remove the birds from the marinade and place them on a lightly greased, shallow baking sheet with a rim. Pour a small amount of the marinade over the birds (just enough to baste). Place the birds in the oven and, roast for 20 to 30 minutes, basting once after 10 minutes.

To make the sauce, put the leftover marinade in a small sauté pan. Bring the marinade to a boil; remove the pan from the heat. Add the butter, and whisk until melted. To serve, place birds on each dinner plate; top with the sauce.

(For inn information see page 174)

Parmesan Chicken

Makes 4 to 6 servings.

This baked cheese- and crumb-coated chicken dish is convenient for picnics, because it is just as good served at room temperature as it is hot out of the oven.

½ cup Dijon mustard
2 to 4 tablespoons white wine
1 cup fresh (soft) bread crumbs (see Carol's Corner below)
1 cup grated Parmesan cheese
3 pounds chicken pieces (thighs work well)

Preheat the oven to 375°F. Grease a baking sheet. In a small bowl, thin the mustard with the wine until a dipping consistency is reached. On a small plate, combine the bread crumbs and cheese. Dip each chicken piece into the mustard mixture, and then roll in the crumb mixture. Place the chicken in a single layer on the prepared baking sheet. Bake the chicken for 45 minutes, or until thoroughly cooked. Serve hot or refrigerate chicken if saving to eat later.

Carol's Corner
Fresh, soft bread crumbs are easily made by placing bread slices (torn into pieces) in a food processor or blender. Process until the bread pieces reach crumb-size. Crumbs may be made ahead and stored in a plastic bag or other tightly covered container in the refrigerator for several days, or in the freezer for longer storage. Do not substitute dry bread crumbs for soft bread crumbs in recipes.

(For inn information see page 74)

Salmon Burgers

Makes 6 servings.

You'll love feasting on these sensational seafood sandwiches topped with Green Tartar Sauce (recipe on page 143). These are a specialty of Chef Trudy Lenzi-Tocco at Elk Cove Inn.

1½ pounds raw salmon fillet, skin and bones (if any) removed
1 red bell pepper, finely diced
1 bunch green onions, thinly sliced (white and green parts)
¼ cup cream or half-and-half
2 eggs
2 teaspoons salt

¼ teaspoon cayenne pepper
1 cup dry bread crumbs
Olive oil or vegetable oil, enough for frying
Green Tartar Sauce (recipe on page 143), for topping
Buns (white or wheat), for serving

Using a sharp knife, chop the salmon fillet into small pieces (using your fingers to help flake the pieces). Place the pieces of salmon in a large bowl. Add the rest of the ingredients, and mix well, adjusting the consistency with bread crumbs, if necessary. Form the salmon mixture into 6 patties. In a large skillet over medium heat, add the oil. When the oil is hot, add the salmon patties, and cook until browned on undersides (2½ to 3 minutes). Turn patties over and cook another 2 to 3 minutes, or until browned and cooked through. Serve on the buns with Green Tartar Sauce.

Make-ahead tip: Patties may be made early in the day and refrigerated until ready to cook.

> **Carol's Corner**
> *These Salmon Burgers were quite a hit at Roxanne and Dennis' cabin when it was my turn to cook at our Faino family reunion. In fact, my mother-in-law, Lorraine, said they were so good she wanted to eat hers without the bun. Other relatives chose to garnish the sandwich with lettuce, tomato, and onion. And the Green Tartar Sauce is simply the best. Salmon Burgers are definitely a new family favorite. Try them.*

(For inn information see page 54)

Vizcaya Mushroom Sauté over Fresh Pasta

Makes 8 servings.

½ plus ¼ cup butter
¼ plus ⅛ cup olive oil
1½ pounds (about 3 medium) yellow onions, cut into ¼-inch slices
    and separated into rings
16 ounces fresh shiitake mushrooms, sliced
8 ounces fresh white button mushrooms, sliced
1 tablespoon dried crushed basil leaves
½ tablespoon dried crushed oregano leaves
1 tablespoon salt
16 ounces any fresh pasta (spirals work well)
8 ounces firm Romano cheese (bulk), sliced and slivered
Chopped fresh parsley or sprigs of fresh basil leaves for garnish

In a large sauté pan over medium-low heat, combine the ¼ cup butter and
the ⅛ cup olive oil. Heat until the butter is melted. Add the separated
onion rings. Stir and cook the onions until they are lightly caramelized
(onions should be light brown in color). In another large sauté pan, combine
the ½ cup butter and the ¼ cup oil. Heat until butter is melted. Add the
mushrooms, basil, and oregano. Sauté until the mushrooms are tender. Add
the cooked onion mixture; stir to combine. Heat thoroughly; keep the
mixture warm over low heat while the pasta is cooking. In a 4-quart kettle,
bring about 3½ quarts water to a boil. Add the salt. Add the pasta, and
cook according to package directions. Drain, and rinse.

To serve, place the pasta on individual plates, and top with the mushroom mixture. Stack slivers of Romano cheese on top in the middle.
Garnish each plate with fresh parsley or fresh basil leaves.

(For inn information see page 92)

Albion River Inn
  Chocolate Mousse
Amy's White Chocolate
  Orange Sugar Cookies
Anderson Creek Apple
  Crumble
Sandy's Apple Pie
Apple Douillons
Apple Pudding
Baked Banana Crumble
Boxcar Billie's Orange
  Cookies
Burnt Blumbleberry
Butterscotch Pecan
  Cookies
Cherries à la Belle
Chocolate Macaroons
Chocolate Peanut Butter
  Cornflake Cookies
Chocolate Walnut
  Cranberry Biscotti
Chocolate-Graham
  Pound Cake
Coconut Carmelized
  Bananas
Crystallized Ginger
  Biscotti

Elk Cove Inn Oatmeal
  Chocolate Chip Cookies
Fresh Fruit Cobbler
Gateau Grieve
Glazed Chocolate
  Zucchini Cake
Grapes La Belle Epoque
Grilled Peaches with
  Raspberry Purée
Heavenly Chocolate Cake
Pear Champagne Sorbet
Poached Pears
Shortbread
Spiced Wine Poached
  Pears
Spicy Baked Pears with
  Vanilla Yogurt
St. Orres Bread Pudding
Strawberry Rhubarb
  Crisp
Stuffed Baked Pears
Sweet & Spicy Candied
  Pecans
Sweet Dream Cookies
White Chocolate Coconut
  Macadamia Cookies

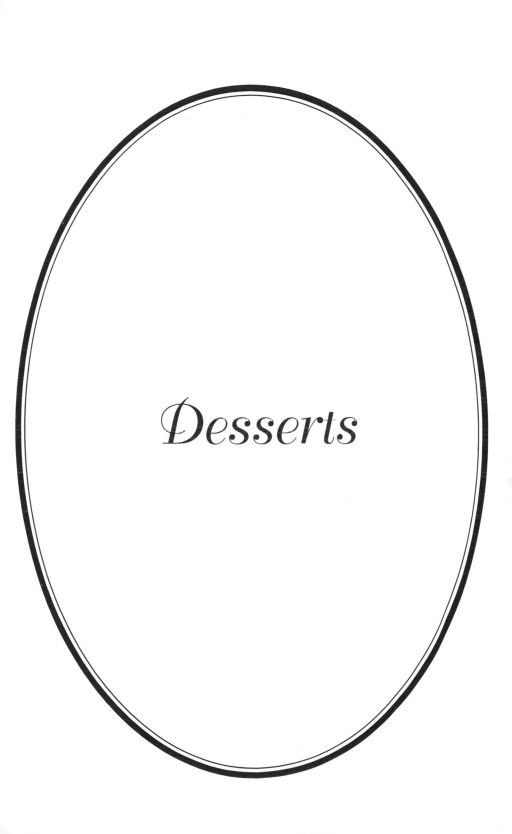

Desserts

Albion River Inn
Chocolate Mousse

Makes 6 to 8 servings.

Love chocolate? Try this.

4 eggs
10 ounces (1⅔ cups) semisweet chocolate chips
1 plus ½ cup heavy cream or whipping cream
¼ cup liqueur of choice (Amaretto, Kahlua, Frangelico, etc.)

Separate the eggs, reserving both the yolks and whites. In a double boiler, heat the chocolate, stirring until melted and smooth. Remove from the heat. In a small saucepan, heat the ½ cup cream with the liqueur until steaming; do not boil. Stir the heated cream/liqueur mixture into the melted chocolate, whisking until smooth. Cool to almost room temperature, then whisk in egg yolks. In a medium bowl, whip the egg whites until soft peaks form. In another bowl, whip the remaining 1 cup cream to peaks, and set aside enough for 6 to 8 small dollops for topping the mousse. With a spatula or spoon, gently fold the whipped cream into the chocolate mixture; then gently fold in the whipped egg whites. Spoon the mousse into a bowl, and let it set up in the refrigerator for an hour. Then scoop the mousse into individual serving dishes or glasses. Chill for several hours until firm. To serve, top each serving of the mousse with a dollop of the whipped cream.

Make-ahead tip: May be made a day or two in advance. Or the mousse may be made up to two weeks in advance and frozen (let thaw in refrigerator overnight before serving).

(For inn information see page 174)

Amy's White Chocolate Orange Sugar Cookies

Makes 4 dozen (3-inch) cookies.

4½ cups all-purpose flour
1½ teaspoons baking soda
½ teaspoon salt
2 cups (4 sticks) unsalted butter, room temperature
1 cup white sugar
1 cup packed brown sugar
2 eggs
3 tablespoons grated orange peel (zest)
2 (11-ounce) packages (or 4 cups) white chocolate morsels

Preheat the oven to 350°F. Set out an ungreased baking sheet. In a large bowl, sift together the flour, baking soda, and salt. In a large bowl, beat the butter with the white and brown sugars until creamy. In a small bowl, beat together the eggs and grated orange peel; add to the butter/sugar mixture. Gradually add the flour mixture to the butter/sugar mixture, one cup at a time, thoroughly combining after each addition. Stir in the chocolate morsels. Drop the dough by heaping tablespoons 2 inches apart on the baking sheet. Bake for 10 to 12 minutes. Transfer the cookies to a wire rack to cool. Store in an airtight container.

Carol's Corner
For a quick and easy way to spoon dough onto the baking sheet, and to have uniformly-sized cookies, try using a #30 ice cream scoop (1³/₄-inch diameter with an easy-trigger release). I use it regularly for making cookies. The scoops are available from kitchen specialty shops and restaurant supply stores.

(For inn information see page 128)

Anderson Creek Apple Crumble

Makes about 8 servings.

A special fruit treat for breakfast. This is not as sweet as dessert crumbles, and it has the added nutritional benefit of oat bran.

½ **cup raisins**
⅓ **cup apple juice**
5 large tart apples, peeled, cored, and chopped
½ **cup brown sugar**
⅓ **cup all-purpose flour**
⅓ **cup oat bran**
½ **cup quick-cooking oatmeal (not instant)**
1 tablespoon cinnamon
1 teaspoon grated lemon peel (zest)
1 teaspoon lemon juice
¼ **cup (½ stick) butter, melted**
Whipped cream

Lightly grease or butter an 8x12-inch glass baking dish. In a small saucepan, gently simmer the raisins in the apple juice for 10 minutes. Spoon the raisins and juice into the prepared dish; add the apples. Preheat the oven to 375°F. In a large bowl, combine the sugar, flour, oat bran, oatmeal, and cinnamon. Add the lemon zest, lemon juice, and melted butter. Stir until mixed and crumbly. Spread evenly over the apple/raisin mixture. Bake, uncovered, for 30 minutes. Spoon into bowls, and top with whipped cream. Serve hot or cold.

(For inn information see page 138)

Sandy's Apple Pie

Makes 8 servings.

Unbaked pastry dough for a 9-inch, double-crust pie
8 cups peeled, cored, and thinly sliced tart apples
1 tablespoon lemon juice
1 cup plus 1 tablespoon sugar
2 tablespoons flour
¾ teaspoon cinnamon
¼ teaspoon nutmeg
¼ teaspoon salt
2 tablespoons butter, cut into small pieces

Preheat the oven to 450°F. Line a 9-inch pie plate with one piece of rolled pastry dough. In a very large bowl, toss the apple slices with the lemon juice. In a small bowl, combine the 1 cup sugar, flour, cinnamon, nutmeg, and salt. Sprinkle the dry mixture over the apples, and stir to mix evenly. Fill the pastry-lined pie plate with the apple mixture (it will be heaping); dot with the butter. Place the second piece of rolled pastry dough over the pie. Fold the overhang under the edge of the bottom crust. Press the 2 crusts together to seal. Using a fork or your fingers, crimp the edge for a decorative finish. With a knife, cut 4 to 6 slits in the top crust (the slits will allow steam to vent during baking). Using a pastry brush, lightly brush the top crust with water. Sprinkle the crust with the remaining 1 tablespoon sugar. Bake for 15 minutes. Reduce the oven temperature to 350°F, and bake for 45 minutes longer. (If the edge of the pie crust is browning too fast, cover the edge with a strip of aluminum foil.) Let the pie cool a bit before cutting. Serve warm or at room temperature. Delicious with whipped cream or ice cream.

(For inn information see page 54)

La Belle Epoque

L ocated in the heart of Napa's historic Old Town, the La Belle Epoque is one of the finest examples of Victorian architecture in California's wine country. This Queen Anne inn boasts thoughtfully appointed accommodations, including a magnificent collection of period antiques, stained glass windows, and Oriental carpets. Local cafes, restaurants, interesting shops, and the Napa Valley Wine Train are within walking distance. Nearby attractions include hot air balloon rides, horseback riding, cycling and hiking trails, golf, tennis, mud baths, and year-round cultural activities.

Breakfast at the La Belle Epoque bed and breakfast inn is a gourmet's delight. Served in the formal dining room or on the intimate porch, home-made specialties include apple douillon in cream, poached pears, Grand Marnier French toast, pork or beef tenderloin, and fresh muffins and lemon scones.

INNKEEPER:	*Georgia Jump*
ADDRESS:	*1386 Calistoga Avenue*
	Napa, CA 94559
TELEPHONE:	*(707) 257-2161; (800) 238-8070*
E-MAIL:	*georgia@labelleepoque.com*
WEBSITE:	*www.labelleepoque.com*
ROOMS:	*6 Rooms; 3 Suites; All with private baths*
CHILDREN:	*Children over the age of 12 are welcome*
ANIMALS:	*Prohibited*

Apple Douillons

Makes 6 servings.

Revel in the compliments when you serve these enticing pastry-wrapped baked apples. La Belle Epoque bed and breakfast serves this house specialty as a gourmet breakfast treat, but it is equally welcomed as a dessert.

6 small Golden Delicious apples
¼ cup plus 6 tablespoons brown sugar
¼ teaspoon cinnamon
⅓ cup currants
4 tablespoons butter, cut into 6 pieces
8 ounces puff pastry, rolled thin
Egg wash (1 egg beaten with 1 teaspoon water)
Heavy cream or whipped cream, optional

Preheat the oven to 375°F. Cover a baking sheet with kitchen parchment paper. Peel the apples. With an apple corer or a melon baller, core the apples (go almost to the bottom, but not quite all the way through). In a small bowl, combine the ¼ cup brown sugar, cinnamon, and currants. Fill the center of each apple with the brown sugar mixture. Top each apple with butter. Roll out the pastry on a lightly floured surface; cut into 6-inch squares (large enough to enclose an apple). Arrange an apple in the center of each square. Brush the edges of the dough with water. Fold the pastry up and around each apple to enclose it, sealing the edges. Pinch the dough together at the very top to seal, leaving a bit of dough sticking up. Brush the pastry with the egg wash (gives color to the dough as it bakes). Arrange the dough-covered apples on the baking sheet. Bake for 45 minutes or until the pastry is golden brown. To serve, place the baked apples in individual bowls, and sprinkle with the remaining 6 tablespoons brown sugar. Add the heavy cream, if desired. To serve as a dessert, place each baked apple on a bed of whipped cream, and sprinkle with more brown sugar.

Apple Pudding

Makes 4 to 6 servings.

This apple delight is a comforting dessert—or it can be served as a special breakfast treat. It's equally delicious topped with whipped cream, ice cream, or half-and-half—your choice. For color, garnish with a bright red strawberry.

¼ **cup (½ stick) butter, room temperature**
¾ **cup sugar**
1 egg
2 cups peeled, chopped apples
1 cup all-purpose flour
1 teaspoon baking powder
1 teaspoon baking soda
¼ **teaspoon cinnamon**
¼ **teaspoon nutmeg**
¼ **teaspoon salt**
Whipped cream, for topping, optional
Ice cream, for topping, optional
Half-and-half, for topping, optional
Fresh strawberries, for garnish, optional

Preheat the oven to 350°F. Coat an 8-inch square baking pan with nonstick cooking spray. In a medium bowl, cream together the butter and sugar. Add the egg and beat well. Stir in the chopped apples. In another medium bowl, sift together the flour, baking powder, baking soda, cinnamon, nutmeg, and salt. Add the dry mixture to the egg/apple mixture. Mix well (batter will be very thick). Spread the batter evenly in the prepared pan. Bake for 40 to 45 minutes or until done. Serve warm or cold, topped and garnished as desired.

(For inn information see page 120)

Baked Banana Crumble

Makes 4 servings.

A sweet, fruit treat for breakfast, or with a scoop of vanilla or cinnamon ice cream atop the baked bananas, it makes an ideal dessert.

4 firm ripe bananas, peeled, cut in half lengthwise, then crosswise
¾ cup orange juice
1 teaspoon vanilla extract
½ cup quick-cooking rolled oats (not instant)
¾ cup packed brown sugar
½ cup all-purpose flour
½ teaspoon cinnamon
½ teaspoon nutmeg
½ teaspoon salt
6 tablespoons chilled butter, cut into small pieces
Half-and-half, for topping, optional
Whipped cream, for topping, optional
Ice cream, for topping, optional

Preheat the oven to 375°F. Butter a 13x9-inch glass baking dish. Place the banana pieces, flat side down, in the bottom of the dish. In a measuring cup, combine the orange juice and vanilla. Pour the mixture over the bananas. In a small bowl, combine the rolled oats, brown sugar, flour, cinnamon, nutmeg, and salt. Using a pastry blender, cut in the butter pieces until mixture is crumbly. Spoon the crumbled mixture over the bananas. Bake for approximately 15 minutes, or until bananas are tender but still firm (do not let them get mushy). Serve warm in individual serving dishes, topped with the half-and-half, whipped cream, or ice cream.

Make-ahead tip: To ease preparation, the crumbled mixture may be made in advance. Cover and refrigerate until ready to use.

(For inn information see page 70)

Boxcar Billie's
Orange Cookies

Makes about 4 dozen.

1 cup (2 sticks) butter or margarine
½ cup white sugar
½ cup packed brown sugar
1 egg, beaten
2 tablespoons orange juice
2 tablespoons grated orange peel (zest)
2½ cups all-purpose flour
1 teaspoon baking soda
½ teaspoon salt
½ to 1 cup chopped nuts

Preheat the oven to 375°F. In a large bowl, beat together the butter or margarine, white sugar, and brown sugar. Beat in the egg, orange juice, and grated orange peel. In a medium bowl, sift together the flour, baking soda, and salt. Add the flour mixture to the beaten mixture. Stir in the nuts. Roll the dough into 1-inch balls, and place on a lightly greased cookie sheet. Using the bottom of a glass that has been dipped in sugar or flour to prevent sticking, flatten the balls to ¼- to ½-inch thickness. Bake for 8 to 9 minutes, or until golden brown. Transfer the cookies to a wire rack to cool. Store in an airtight container. These cookies freeze well.

(For inn information see page 28)

Burnt Blumbleberry

Makes about 18 servings.

The Jabberwock bed and breakfast inn accompanies its baked custard (topped with raspberries) with warm croissants, coffee, and its famous Jabberjuice. It's special for breakfast, but Burnt Blumbleberry also makes a great dessert. Plan ahead, since it must be made in advance.

15 egg yolks
1½ cups sugar
8 plus 3½ cups cream
3 tablespoons vanilla extract

18 teaspoons sugar
Blumbleberry Sauce
(ingredients and directions below)

Preheat the oven to 350°F. Set out 18 ungreased ramekins (1-cup size or slightly smaller). In a mixer or a blender, combine the egg yolks, sugar, and the 3½ cups cream; continue to blend on low speed while heating the remaining 8 cups cream in a large saucepan. Heat the cream to scalding (just below the boiling point). Slowly pour the hot cream into the egg yolk mixture, blending continuously. Stir in the vanilla. Strain the custard mixture into a pitcher. Pour the mixture into the ramekins, filling each ¾ full. Place the ramekins in two large baking pans (or roasting pans), leaving a little space between ramekins. Pour hot water into the pans to about halfway up the sides of the ramekins (the water bath helps the custard to bake evenly). Bake for 45 minutes, each batch separately (or in two ovens). Remove from the oven; let custards cool in the water bath. Remove the ramekins from the water; cover, and refrigerate overnight, or for up to 4 days (custard will firm). To serve, bring the custards to room temperature. Sprinkle the top of each with 1 teaspoon sugar. Place the ramekins on a cookie sheet, and broil until the sugar is browned. Let stand a few minutes before serving warm, or chill to serve cold later. Top with the Blumbleberry Sauce before serving.

Blumbleberry sauce:
1 (12-ounce) bag frozen raspberries
½ cup sugar

About 1 hour before serving, gently mix the raspberries and sugar. Spoon a tablespoon of the berry mixture over each custard right before serving.

(For inn information see page 166)

Butterscotch Pecan Cookies

Makes about 4 dozen cookies.

6 tablespoons butter, room temperature
⅔ cup packed brown sugar
1 egg
½ teaspoon vanilla extract
1¼ cups all-purpose flour
½ teaspoon baking powder
¼ teaspoon salt
½ cup finely chopped pecans

In a large bowl, beat together the butter and brown sugar. Add the egg and vanilla, and beat well. In a medium bowl, sift together the flour, baking powder, and salt. Gradually add the sifted dry ingredients to the egg/brown sugar mixture. Stir in the pecans. Shape into 2 rolls (7 inches each), and wrap each in plastic wrap. Refrigerate for 2 hours, or until firm. Preheat the oven to 350°F. Set out an ungreased baking sheet. Unwrap the dough, and cut into ¼-inch slices. Place the slices 2 inches apart on the baking sheet. Bake for 10 to 12 minutes, or until the edges of the cookies begin to brown. Remove the cookies to a wire rack to cool. Store in an airtight container. These cookies freeze well.

(For inn information see page 178)

Cherries à la Belle

Makes 12 servings.

1 (20-ounce) can crushed pineapple in natural juice, undrained
1 (20-ounce) can tart cherries, undrained
1 (18¼-ounce) lemon cake mix without pudding in the mix
1 cup (2 sticks) butter, melted
½ cup chopped pecans
Grated peel (zest) of 1 lemon
Heavy cream, for serving

Preheat the oven to 350°F. Coat a 13x9-inch baking dish with a nonstick cooking spray. Spread the can of pineapple evenly into the baking dish. Next, spread the can of cherries evenly into the baking dish. Sprinkle the box of dry cake mix evenly on top of the fruit. DO NOT MIX. Pour the melted butter over the top of the cake mix. Sprinkle the nuts and lemon zest over the top. Bake for 50 minutes. Serve hot with the heavy cream.

Carol's Corner
Keep the ingredients for this recipe in your pantry and you'll be ready at a moment's notice to bake dessert for a party of 12. This dessert is also good served with whipped cream or ice cream. Garnish each serving with a lemon peel curl or grated lemon zest. Lemon zest can be grated ahead of time and kept in a plastic bag in the freezer.

(For inn information see page 202)

Forest Manor

Discriminating visitors to Napa Valley find the Forest Manor bed and breakfast provides privacy, tranquility, natural beauty, and a restful atmosphere. Complemented by beautiful architecture, this romantic getaway reflects the magic of California's wine country. Tucked among the forest and vineyards of Napa Valley, it features massive carved beams, large windows, high vaulted ceilings, and a fifty-three foot pool. The spacious air-conditioned suites provide privacy and rest for guests.

Nearby points of interest include Lake Berryessa, the Culinary Institute, Old Faithful Geyser, and world class restaurants and wineries.

The full gourmet breakfast, with a daily changing menu, features only the freshest ingredients available.

INNKEEPERS:	*Peter & Monica Lilly; Greg & Debra Winters, Owners*
ADDRESS:	*415 Cold Springs Road* *Angwin, CA 94508*
TELEPHONE:	*(707) 965-3538; (800) 788-0364*
E-MAIL:	*innkeepers@forestmanor.com*
WEBSITE:	*www.forestmanor.com*
ROOMS:	*6 Suites; All with private baths*
CHILDREN:	*Children over the age of 16 are welcome*
ANIMALS:	*Prohibited*

Chocolate Macaroons

Makes about 2 dozen cookies.

Parchment paper used to line the baking sheet in this cookie recipe has a nonstick surface and makes cleanup easier. Look for parchment paper in your favorite grocery store or in kitchenware shops.

2 egg whites
1 cup sugar
¼ teaspoon salt
½ teaspoon vanilla extract
1½ squares unsweetened chocolate, melted and cooled
1½ cups shredded coconut

Preheat the oven to 325°F. Cover a baking sheet with kitchen parchment paper. In a medium bowl, beat the egg whites until foamy. Gradually add the sugar, a few spoonfuls at a time, blending after each addition. Continue beating the egg whites on high speed until they form peaks with tips that stand straight when the beaters are lifted. Add the salt and vanilla, then fold in cooled, melted chocolate and the coconut. Drop the cookie mixture by teaspoonfuls onto the prepared baking sheet. Bake for about 15 minutes or until done. (The tops should look dry, but slightly moist between cracks. Do not overcook, or they will be hard.) Cool on the parchment paper for 15 minutes, then remove the cookies with a metal spatula. Store the cookies in an airtight container.

Chocolate Peanut Butter Cornflake Cookies

Makes about 3 dozen.

It doesn't get any easier than this—only 3 ingredients, and no baking required.

1 (12-ounce) package (or 2 cups) chocolate chips
¾ cup creamy peanut butter
4 cups cornflakes

In a large saucepan, on low heat, melt the chips and peanut butter, stirring constantly until blended and smooth. Remove from the heat and add the cornflakes. Stir until the cornflakes are well coated with the chocolate/peanut butter mixture. Using a tablespoon, drop the cookies onto a piece of waxed paper. The cookies will take a few hours to set, or they may be placed in the refrigerator to speed-up setting. Cookies may also be stored in refrigerator.

Variations: Butterscotch chips may be substituted for chocolate chips. Chunky peanut butter may be substituted for creamy peanut butter.

(For inn information see page 72)

Chocolate Walnut Cranberry Biscotti

Makes 32 cookies.

2 cups all-purpose flour
1 cup sugar
½ teaspoon baking powder
½ teaspoon baking soda
½ teaspoon salt
½ teaspoon ground cinnamon
¼ teaspoon ground cloves
¼ cup plus 1 tablespoon strong-brewed coffee, cooled
4 teaspoons milk
1 large egg
1 teaspoon vanilla extract
¾ cup chopped walnuts
1¼ cups semisweet chocolate chips
¾ cup dried cranberries

Preheat the oven to 350°F. In a large bowl, combine the flour, sugar, baking powder, baking soda, salt, cinnamon, and cloves. Blend well. In a small bowl, whisk together the coffee, the milk, egg, and vanilla. Add the liquid ingredients to the dry ingredients, blending well with a mixer. Add the walnuts, chocolate chips, and dried cranberries. Divide the dough in half. On a well-floured board, form each portion of dough into a flat log, measuring ½ inch high x 3½ inches wide. Grease and flour a cookie sheet. Place the logs about 4 inches apart on the prepared cookie sheet. Bake for 20 to 25 minutes, until cake-like. Cool. Reduce the oven temperature to 300°F. With a serrated knife, cut each log diagonally into ½-inch slices. Lay the slices flat on the cookie sheet, and bake for another 6 to 8 minutes. Cool and serve. For harder biscotti, cook the slices on both sides for 6 to 8 minutes. Recipe can easily be doubled.

(For inn information see page 24)

Chocolate-Graham Pound Cake with Toasted Almonds & Chantilly Cream

Makes 6 generous or 12 small servings.

Pound cake:

6 ounces (1½ sticks) butter, room temperature
½ cup packed brown sugar
1 cup white sugar
1 teaspoon vanilla extract
3 eggs
¾ cup unsweetened cocoa powder
1 cup graham flour (coarsely ground whole-wheat flour)
¼ teaspoon baking powder

½ teaspoon salt
3 plus 6 tablespoons (about ⅔ cup) whole milk
½ plus ½ cup sliced almonds, toasted and chopped

Chantilly cream:
½ cup heavy cream
2 tablespoons sugar
1 teaspoon vanilla extract

To make pound cake, preheat the oven to 350°F. Generously grease and flour a 9x5-inch loaf pan. In a large bowl, combine the butter, brown sugar, white sugar, and vanilla; beat until creamy. Add the eggs, 1 at a time, beating well after each addition. In a medium bowl, sift together the cocoa powder, graham flour, baking powder, and salt. Add one quarter of the dry ingredients to the wet ingredients and blend. Add 3 tablespoons of the milk and blend. Continue to add the dry ingredients alternating with the remaining milk, ending with the last one-quarter of the dry ingredients. Fold in ½ cup almonds. Spoon the batter into the prepared pan, and tap the pan gently to release any air pockets. Sprinkle the remaining ½ cup almonds over the top. Bake about 1 hour or until done. Cool 10 minutes, and remove the cake from the pan. Cut into slices, and serve warm.

To make the Chantilly cream, in a small, deep bowl, beat the heavy cream until soft peaks form. Add the sugar and vanilla, and beat until smooth. Serve cake slices on dessert plates. Top with the Chantilly cream.

Note: The cake is also good with vanilla ice cream and hot fudge sauce.

(For inn information see page 160)

Coconut Caramelized Bananas

Makes 4 servings.

¼ cup packed light brown sugar
2 tablespoons water
2 large bananas, peeled and
quartered (cut crosswise and
lengthwise)
⅛ cup rum
¼ cup canned, unsweetened
coconut milk (see Carol's
Corner)
4 scoops vanilla ice cream

Chocolate sauce:
⅔ cup semisweet chocolate
chips
½ cup cream

Toasted coconut, for garnish
(see directions below)

In a small sauté pan, combine the brown sugar and water. Bring to a boil, and reduce by half. Add the bananas, and cook for 1 minute. Sprinkle with the rum; heat for 1 minute and flambé. (To flambé, use a long wooden match, and carefully ignite the mixture.) When flames subside, add the coconut milk, and cook until the sauce has thickened slightly. To serve, place 2 banana pieces on each of 4 small dessert plates (or use shallow bowls). Add some sauce from the pan and a scoop of ice cream. Top with the chocolate sauce, and garnish with toasted coconut.

To make the chocolate sauce, combine the chocolate chips and cream in a heavy saucepan. Heat gently to melt the chocolate, and stir until smooth. Keep warm over low heat until ready to pour over the bananas and ice cream. Refrigerate any leftover sauce. Chocolate sauce may be reheated in the microwave. (Check and stir after every 20 seconds until warm.)

To prepare the toasted coconut, preheat the oven to 350°F. Spread ⅓ cup shredded coconut on an ungreased baking sheet. Bake for 3 minutes. Stir and bake an additional minute. Stir and continue baking 1 or 2 more minutes, watching carefully, until lightly browned. (May be made in advance.)

> **Carol's Corner**
> *You'll want to make this fabulous dessert more than once. Leftover canned coconut milk can be refrigerated in an airtight container for up to a week, or frozen for longer storage (up to 6 months).*

(For inn information see page 174)

Crystallized Ginger Biscotti

Makes 36 cookies.

2 cups all-purpose flour
1½ teaspoons baking powder
1 teaspoon ground ginger
¼ teaspoon salt
⅔ cup sugar
½ cup (1 stick) butter, room temperature
2 large eggs
1 teaspoon vanilla extract
⅔ cup finely chopped crystallized ginger slices or chunks
½ cup finely chopped toasted almonds
½ cup white chocolate chips or white morsels

Preheat the oven to 325°F. Grease and flour a large baking sheet. Set out an ungreased baking sheet. In a small bowl, combine the flour, baking powder, ground ginger and salt. In a large bowl, with an electric mixer on medium speed, beat together the sugar and butter until light and fluffy. Beat in the eggs and vanilla. Reduce the mixer speed, and gradually add the flour mixture until well combined. With a spoon, stir in the crystallized ginger, almonds, and chips. Divide the dough into 3 equal portions. On a floured surface, shape each portion into a 10-inch log and place 2 inches apart on the prepared baking sheet. Flatten each log slightly to about ¾-inch thickness. Bake the logs for 20 to 25 minutes or until lightly browned. Leaving the logs on the baking sheet, cool on a wire rack for at least 15 minutes. Carefully transfer logs to a cutting board. Using a serrated knife and a sawing motion, cut each log diagonally into 12 slices. Lay the slices flat, about ½ inch apart, on an ungreased baking sheet. Bake 10 minutes longer to dry the slices. Transfer slices to wire racks to cool completely. (The biscotti will harden as they cool.) Store in an airtight container.

(For inn information see page 40)

Elk Cove Inn Oatmeal Chocolate Chip Cookies

Makes 8 dozen cookies.

These yummy, crunchy yet chewy, cookies are best slightly undercooked and warm from the oven. This is a large recipe, and because the dough keeps well in the refrigerator, you can have freshly baked cookies anytime in a mere 15 minutes.

2 cups (4 sticks) butter, room temperature
2 cups white sugar
2 cups packed brown sugar
4 eggs
2 teaspoons vanilla extract
4 cups all-purpose flour
2 teaspoons baking powder
2 teaspoons baking soda
2 teaspoons salt
1 (12-ounce) package (or 2 cups) semisweet chocolate chips
3 cups chopped nuts
2 cups old-fashioned rolled oats
3 cups granola, plain or with dried fruit (homemade or purchased)
Grated orange peel (zest), to taste

Preheat the oven to 375°F. Set out an ungreased baking sheet. In a large bowl, combine the butter, sugar, and brown sugar until creamy. Beat in the eggs and vanilla. In a medium bowl, sift together the flour, baking powder, baking soda, and salt. Add the flour mixture to the creamed mixture. Stir in the chocolate chips, nuts, rolled oats, granola, and orange zest. Mix well. Roll the dough into large balls (golf ball-size). Place 2 inches apart on the baking sheet. Bake for 8 to 10 minutes or until barely golden. Cool cookies for 2 to 3 minutes; then transfer them to a wire rack. Enjoy the cookies warm.

(For inn information see page 54)

Fresh Fruit Cobbler

Makes 8 servings.

Fresh apples, peaches, cherries, blueberries or blackberries—all would be good choices for this cobbler recipe. Frozen fruit may be substituted if fresh is not available.

⅔ to 1 cup sugar, depending on sweetness of fruit
1 tablespoon cornstarch
1 cup water
3 cups fresh fruit, sliced (except for berries), including any juice
2 tablespoons butter, cut into small pieces
Cinnamon
1 cup all-purpose flour
1 tablespoon sugar
1½ teaspoons baking powder
½ teaspoon salt
3 tablespoons shortening
½ cup milk
Cream, whipped cream, or ice cream, for topping

Preheat the oven to 400°F. Set out a 1½-quart, ungreased baking dish. In a large saucepan, combine the sugar and cornstarch. Gradually stir in the water. Bring mixture to a boil. Stirring constantly, boil for 1 minute. Add the fruit and any juice. Carefully pour the fruit mixture into the baking dish. Dot with the butter, and sprinkle with cinnamon to taste. In a medium bowl, sift together the flour, sugar, baking powder, and salt. Using a pastry blender, cut in the shortening until the mixture resembles coarse crumbs. Stir in the milk until just combined. Drop the batter by spoonfuls randomly onto the hot fruit. Bake, uncovered, for 25 to 30 minutes or until biscuits are browned and the fruit is bubbling. Cool slightly, and serve warm with cream, whipped cream, or ice cream.

Note: To serve later, the cobbler may be completely cooled after baking. Reheat, if desired.

(For inn information see page 88)

Gateau Grieve

Makes 2 loaf cakes.

Interestingly enough, this cake recipe uses no dairy products. Perfect for the vegan in your life.

4 to 5 apples, peeled, cored, and diced
1 cup raisins
3 cups sugar
2 cups water
1 cup oil
2 tablespoons unsweetened cocoa powder
4 cups all-purpose flour
3½ teaspoons baking soda
Pinch of salt
1 teaspoon cinnamon
½ teaspoon ground allspice
1 cup miniature semisweet chocolate chips
1 cup chopped nuts

Preheat the oven to 350°F. Grease and flour two 9x5-inch loaf pans. Line the bottom of the pans with waxed paper. Grease and flour the waxed paper. In a very large saucepan, combine the apples, raisins, sugar, water, oil, and cocoa. Bring to a boil, and boil for 3 minutes (watch so it doesn't boil over). Remove from the heat, and let the mixture cool to lukewarm. In a large bowl, sift together the flour, baking soda, salt, cinnamon, and allspice. Add the dry mixture to the cooled apple mixture along with the miniature chocolate chips and nuts. Stir until well combined. Divide the batter evenly into the prepared loaf pans. Bake for 1 hour or longer until the cakes spring back when lightly pressed with your finger. Remove the pans from the oven, and place them on a wire rack for 15 minutes to cool. Remove the cakes from the pans, and peel off the waxed paper from the bottom of each. Finish cooling the cakes on the wire rack. Store at room temperature, or freeze.

(For inn information see page 30)

Glazed Chocolate Zucchini Cake

Makes 1 large Bundt cake.

Cake:
¾ cup (1½ sticks) butter, room temperature
2 cups sugar
3 eggs
2 teaspoons vanilla extract
1 tablespoon grated orange peel (zest)
2 cups (or about 2 medium) grated raw zucchini
2¾ cups all-purpose flour
½ cup unsweetened cocoa powder
2½ teaspoons baking powder

1½ teaspoons baking soda
1 teaspoon salt
1 teaspoon cinnamon
½ cup milk
1 cup chopped walnuts

Lemon orange glaze:
1 cup powdered sugar
1 teaspoon vanilla extract
1 to 2 teaspoons grated orange peel (zest)
4 to 6 teaspoons lemon juice

To make the cake, preheat the oven to 350°F. Grease and flour a 10-inch diameter Bundt pan. In a large bowl, combine the butter and sugar, beating until smooth. Beat in the eggs; mix thoroughly. Stir in the vanilla, orange zest, and grated zucchini; blend well. In a medium bowl, sift together the flour, cocoa, baking powder, baking soda, salt, and cinnamon. Add to the zucchini mixture alternately with the milk; beat until well mixed. Stir in the walnuts. Pour the batter into the prepared pan. Bake for 1 hour, or until a toothpick inserted comes out clean. Let cool in the pan for 30 to 40 minutes. Remove from the pan; cool completely.

To make the glaze, combine in a small bowl the powdered sugar, vanilla, and orange zest. Add enough lemon juice to make a glaze of drizzling consistency. Drizzle over the cooled cake.

(For inn information see page 126)

Grapes La Belle Epoque

Makes 4 servings.

Colorful red and green grapes, tossed in a flavorful sweet syrup, served in ripe melon halves—what a beautiful and unique presentation.

⅓ **cup sugar**
⅓ **cup dry white wine**
2 tablespoons water
1 tablespoon finely chopped fresh rosemary leaves
1 tablespoon lime juice
1 pound seedless red and/or green grapes, washed, stems removed
2 small ripe cantaloupes, cut in half, seeds removed
4 dollops sour cream, for garnish, optional
Chopped rosemary flowers, for garnish, optional
Grated lime peel, for garnish, optional

In a one-quart saucepan, heat the sugar, wine, water, and rosemary leaves to boiling over medium heat. Reduce the heat to low and simmer 10 minutes. Remove from the heat; stir in the lime juice. Strain the syrup. Cover and refrigerate for several hours. To serve, toss the grapes with the chilled rosemary syrup. Check each cantaloupe half to see that it sits straight on a plate (if it isn't level, cut a small piece off the bottom). Spoon the grapes and syrup into the middle of each cantaloupe half. If desired, garnish with a small dollop of sour cream, and sprinkle with the chopped rosemary flowers or grated lime peel. Serve immediately.

Variation: Instead of using the cantaloupes as serving bowls, use a melon baller to make cantaloupe balls. Mix them with the grapes and syrup. Divide the fruit and syrup evenly among stemmed glasses. Garnish as desired. Just as wonderful this way, they are a little easier to eat.

Make-ahead tip: The syrup may be made a day in advance.

(For inn information see page 202)

Grilled Peaches with Raspberry Purée

Makes 4 servings.

And you thought the charcoal grill was for steak and chicken only. Try these grilled peaches with a scoop of vanilla ice cream on the side.

5 ounces frozen raspberries in light syrup, partially thawed (use half a 10-ounce package)
1½ teaspoons lemon juice
2 medium fresh, ripe peaches, peeled, halved, and pitted
1½ tablespoons brown sugar
¼ teaspoon ground cinnamon
1½ teaspoons rum flavoring
1½ teaspoons butter
Ice cream, optional

In a food processor or blender, whirl the raspberries and lemon juice together until smooth to make a purée. Strain the purée and discard the seeds. Cover the raspberry purée and chill. Cut 1 sheet (18x18 inches) of heavy-duty aluminum foil. Place the four peach halves, cut side up, on the foil. In a small bowl, combine the brown sugar and cinnamon; spoon evenly into the center of each peach half. Sprinkle with the rum flavoring, and dot with butter. Fold foil over the peaches, and loosely seal. Place the grill rack over medium coals. Place the peach bundle on the rack. Cook 15 minutes, or until the peaches are thoroughly heated. To serve, place the grilled peach halves on small dessert plates, and spoon 2 tablespoons of raspberry purée over each. Add a scoop of ice cream, if desired.

(For inn information see page 40)

Heavenly Chocolate Cake

Makes 1 large Bundt cake.

This is a moist, dense cake with a very mild chocolate flavor. Because of its richness, it does not need any icing. If desired, serve with ice cream or whipped cream.

1 cup (2 sticks) butter
½ cup shortening
3 cups sugar
5 eggs
3 cups all-purpose flour
½ teaspoon salt
4 tablespoons unsweetened cocoa powder
1 cup milk
1 tablespoon vanilla extract
Powdered sugar for dusting, optional
Ice cream or whipped cream, optional

Preheat the oven to 325°F. Grease and flour a 12-cup Bundt or tube pan. In a large bowl, beat together the butter, shortening, and sugar at high speed until light and fluffy. Add the eggs, one at a time, beating well after each addition. In a medium bowl, sift together the flour, salt, and cocoa powder. Add the dry ingredients, alternating with the milk, to the wet ingredients, beating after each addition and ending with the dry ingredients. Add the vanilla, and mix well. Pour the batter into the prepared pan. Bake for 60 to 70 minutes, or until a wooden skewer inserted in the center comes out clean. Cool the cake in the pan on a wire rack for 15 minutes. Remove the cake from the pan, and finish cooling on the wire rack. For a beautiful presentation, dust with powdered sugar, and top with ice cream or whipped cream, if desired.

(For inn information see page 162)

Pear Champagne Sorbet

Makes 8 servings.

Top the warm Stuffed Baked Pears (recipe on page 231) with this unique pear sorbet. Another time, try serving the sorbet in colorful, individual dessert cups to accompany a plateful of your favorite cookies.

5 pears, peeled, cored, and cut into cubes
1 cup champagne
2 tablespoons Pear de Pear (pear liqueur)
¾ cup sugar
½ teaspoon freshly grated nutmeg
1 teaspoon fresh lemon juice
1 cup heavy cream

In a large saucepan, combine the pears, champagne, liqueur, sugar, nutmeg, and lemon juice, and simmer until the pears are soft and the alcohol has evaporated (about 10 to 15 minutes). Transfer the mixture to a food processor, and blend until smooth. Let the mixture cool to room temperature. Add the heavy cream; mix well. Freeze the mixture in an ice cream machine, following manufacturer's instructions. Store the sorbet in the freezer.

(For inn information see page 150)

Poached Pears

Makes 4 servings.

The "red hots" lend flavor, as well as color, to this warm and beautiful breakfast treat.

3 cups apple cider
1 cup red hot cinnamon candies
4 ripe, firm pears, peeled and cored
Whipped cream, for serving

In a large saucepan, combine the apple cider and cinnamon candies. Cook over medium heat, stirring occasionally, until the candies are dissolved. Add the pears to the cider/cinnamon mixture. Cover the pan, and simmer pears for 25 to 30 minutes, occasionally basting with the juice. To serve, spoon the warm pears into individual serving dishes with several spoonfuls of juice. Top with the whipped cream.

Make-ahead tip: Pears may be made a day in advance and refrigerated. When ready to serve, gently reheat on the stovetop or in the microwave.

(For inn information see page 70)

Shortbread

Makes about 36 cookies.

Guests at the Mangels House rave about these tender-crisp, butter-rich cookies, and enjoy them with port, sherry, or a cup of tea.

1 cup (2 sticks) butter
¾ cup sugar (use a combination of half white and half brown)
2½ cups all-purpose flour

Preheat the oven to 325°F. In a food processor, cream the butter with the sugar. Add the flour, and process until the ingredients just begin to hold together. Press the dough evenly into an ungreased 13x9-inch baking pan. With a fork, prick the dough all over, either in an even-row pattern or randomly. With a knife, score the dough (cut the surface, not all the way through) into rectangular, triangular or square cookie-size pieces. Chill the dough for 30 minutes before baking. Bake for 20 to 25 minutes, or until the edges begin to brown. Remove the pan, and turn off the oven. While the shortbread is still hot, using a knife, cut the shortbread into cookies, following your score lines and leaving them in the pan. Return the pan to the oven, and leave the door ajar. Keep the shortbread in the oven until the pan is completely cooled. Remove the cookies from the pan; store in an airtight container.

(For inn information see page 50)

Spiced Wine Poached Pears

Makes 8 servings.

These beautiful, reddish-purple, poached pears look elegant served in individual stemmed glassware. Spoon the hot syrupy sauce over the pears and garnish each serving with an edible flower.

2 cups Merlot or other red wine
2 tablespoons lemon juice
1 cup sugar
1 cinnamon stick
6 whole cloves
1 vanilla bean
Grated peel (zest) of 1 lemon
8 firm ripe pears (with stems attached)
Edible flowers, for garnish, optional
Mint leaves, for garnish, optional

In a deep saucepan, combine the wine, lemon juice, sugar, cinnamon stick, cloves, vanilla bean (split the bean lengthwise and scrape out the tiny seeds—add the bean and seeds), lemon zest, and enough water to cover the pears. Bring the mixture to a boil. Meanwhile, peel the pears without removing the stems. Lower the heat under the saucepan, and carefully place the pears in the hot liquid mixture. Simmer very slowly until pears are just tender, about 45 to 60 minutes. Remove the pears to a large serving dish, or to individual serving dishes. Rapidly reduce the remaining liquid to measure about 1 cup. Strain the liquid, and pour over the pears. Garnish with edible flowers and mint leaves, if desired. Serve hot.

Carol's Corner
I also tried this recipe cutting the pears in half and coring them completely (great for smaller servings and ease of eating). The pears may be made in advance, covered and refrigerated. Reheat gently before serving. I discovered the pears are also delicious cold.

(For inn information see page 202)

Spicy Baked Pears with Vanilla Yogurt

Makes 8 servings.

Try this award-winning fruit dish from Joshua Grindle Inn. Use pears that are ripe, yet still firm, for best results.

1 cup packed dark brown sugar
Ground cinnamon
Ground mace
Ground cloves
4 large ripe pears, peeled, halved, and cored
1½ cups orange juice
½ cup (1 stick) chilled butter, cut into small pieces
8 dollops of vanilla yogurt, for topping
Freshly grated nutmeg, for garnish

Preheat the oven to 350°F. Coat a 13x9-inch glass baking dish with nonstick cooking spray. Line the bottom of the baking dish with the brown sugar. Sprinkle the brown sugar layer generously with cinnamon to taste. With a lighter touch, sprinkle with mace and cloves to taste. Lay the pear halves, cut side down, on the sugar mixture (if the spices are sprinkled on top of the pears, the cinnamon will burn). Pour the orange juice over the pears. Dot with the butter. Bake for 20 minutes, or until the pears are tender. To serve, place a pear half, cut side down, in each of eight small dishes. Pour some of the brown sugar/orange juice mixture over the pears, and top each half with a dollop of vanilla yogurt. Garnish with freshly grated nutmeg.

(For inn information see page 126)

St. Orres Bread Pudding

Makes 12 servings.

Bread pudding is usually served as a dessert, often with a special sauce or ice cream. This version can be dressed up for dessert, or served as is for a warm and wonderful breakfast treat.

3 cups milk
3 cups heavy cream
1 (16-ounce) loaf sweet French bread (such as Hawaiian Sweet Bread)
11 eggs
1¾ cups sugar
⅛ cup vanilla extract
¼ cup dark rum
1 cup dried cherries
1 cup raisins or currants
1 cup slivered almonds
1 teaspoon cinnamon
Nutmeg, for garnish

Preheat the oven to 325°F. Coat a 13x9-inch glass baking dish with nonstick cooking spray. In a very large bowl, combine the milk and cream. Cut the loaf of bread into 1-inch cubes. Add the bread cubes to the milk/cream mixture. Let the bread soak for about 30 minutes. In a large bowl, beat together the eggs, sugar, vanilla, and rum. Add to the soaked bread mixture. Then fold in the remaining ingredients, and combine thoroughly. Spoon the mixture into the prepared baking dish. Bake for 1¼ to 1½ hours, or until a knife inserted in center comes out clean. Cool on a wire rack for about 20 minutes before serving. The bread pudding may be served warm or refrigerated to serve cold later.

(For inn information see page 36)

Strawberry Rhubarb Crisp

Makes about 8 servings.

Filling:
2 pounds fresh strawberries, washed, stemmed and cut in half
2 pounds fresh rhubarb, cleaned and cut into bite-size pieces
2 cups sugar
½ cup all-purpose flour

Crumb topping:
1 cup packed brown sugar
1 cup all-purpose flour
½ teaspoon cinnamon
½ cup (1 stick) chilled butter, cut into small pieces
Whipped cream or vanilla ice cream, for topping
Fresh mint sprigs, for garnish

Preheat the oven to 350°F. Coat a 13x9-inch baking dish with nonstick cooking spray. In a very large bowl, gently combine the strawberries and rhubarb with the sugar and flour. Transfer the filling to the prepared baking dish. To make the crumb topping, in a small bowl, combine the brown sugar, flour, and cinnamon. Using a pastry blender (or two knives used scissor-fashion), cut in the butter until the mixture resembles coarse crumbs. Sprinkle the crumb topping over the strawberry/rhubarb mixture. Bake for approximately 1½ hours, or until bubbly and topping is golden brown. (Start checking after 1 hour and 15 minutes.) Let cool on a wire rack for about 15 minutes before serving. Serve warm with either a dollop of whipped cream or a scoop of the ice cream. Garnish with the mint sprigs.

(For inn information see page 98)

Stuffed Baked Pears with Vanilla Sauce & Pear Champagne Sorbet

Makes 8 servings.

A guest at Oak Knoll Inn in Napa remarked, "I knew we were at the right place when we started the day with dessert." Here is the recipe for the breakfast fruit course that got such a rave review. The recipes for the accompaniments, Vanilla Sauce and Pear Champagne Sorbet, are on pages 151 and 224. Both should be prepared in advance.

4 ripe firm pears, peeled, cut in half, and cored
Fresh lemon juice
½ cup raisins
¼ cup sugar
2 tablespoons butter
2 tablespoons brandy
2 teaspoons cinnamon

½ teaspoon freshly grated nutmeg
8 mint leaves, for garnish
Vanilla Sauce, for serving (recipe on page 151)
Pear Champagne Sorbet, for serving (recipe on page 224)

Preheat the oven to 400°F. Butter a 13x9-inch glass baking dish. Cut a thin slice off the back of each pear half to make it sit flat. Rub each with the lemon juice to prevent discoloration. Place the pear halves close together in the baking dish, cored side up. In a food processor or blender, combine the raisins, sugar, butter, brandy, cinnamon, and nutmeg until finely chopped and well mixed. Stuff the pear halves generously with the raisin mixture. Cover the baking dish loosely with foil. Bake the pears for 30 minutes. On each of 8 small plates, arrange one warm pear half on a pool of vanilla sauce. Garnish with a mint sprig at the stem end. Add a dollop of pear sorbet on top—a nice contrast to the warm pear.

(For inn information see page 150)

Sweet & Spicy Candied Pecans

Makes 1½ cups candied pecans.

These candied pecans are a novel topping for the Waldorf Salad on page 163. Simply eaten out-of-hand, they make a wonderful snack.

3 tablespoons light corn syrup
1½ tablespoons sugar
¾ teaspoon salt
¼ teaspoon (generous) freshly ground black pepper
⅛ teaspoon cayenne pepper
1½ cups pecan pieces

Preheat the oven to 325°F. Coat a baking sheet with nonstick cooking spray. In a large bowl, combine the corn syrup, sugar, salt, black pepper, and cayenne pepper. Stir to blend. Add the pecan pieces; stir gently to coat. Transfer the mixture to the prepared baking sheet. Bake the pecans for 5 minutes. Remove the pecans from the oven; using a fork, stir to coat the pecans with the melted spice mixture. Return the pecans to the oven. Continue baking until the nuts are golden and the coating bubbles, about 10 minutes. Place a large piece of aluminum foil on a work surface. Transfer the pecans to the foil. Working quickly, separate the nuts with a fork. Cool completely before storing in an airtight container. The candied pecans can be stored at room temperature for several weeks. They may also be refrigerated or frozen.

(For inn information see page 162)

Sweet Dream Cookies

Makes 5 dozen cookies.

Make the dough for these delicious cookies at least two hours before you want to bake them, since the dough needs to be chilled and firm. For convenience, the dough can be prepared and refrigerated a day in advance.

1 cup (2 sticks) unsalted butter, room temperature
1½ cups packed brown sugar
1 egg, room temperature
1 teaspoon vanilla extract
2½ cups unbleached all-purpose flour
1 teaspoon baking soda
1 teaspoon cinnamon
1 teaspoon ground ginger
½ teaspoon salt
1 (12-ounce) package semisweet chocolate chips
1 cup chopped walnuts
1 cup powdered sugar

In a large bowl, beat together the butter, brown sugar, egg, and vanilla. Sift together the flour, baking soda, cinnamon, ginger, and salt. Blend the dry mixture into the butter mixture. Stir in the chocolate chips and walnuts. Refrigerate until firm. Preheat the oven to 375°F. Lightly grease a baking sheet. Break off small pieces of the dough; roll between your palms into 1-inch balls. Dredge the balls of dough in the powdered sugar. Place on prepared baking sheet, spacing at least 2 inches apart. Bake for 10 minutes (the cookies will not look done). Let cool 5 minutes on a baking sheet. Transfer the cookies to a wire rack to cool. Store in an airtight container.

(For inn information see page 94)

Vintners Inn

S et amidst a forty-five-acre vineyard in the heart of Sonoma wine country, the Vintners Inn has been planned to the finest detail and carefully created to provide a blend of allure and personal service. With the buildings encircling a central plaza, the inn is surrounded by relaxing views of lush vineyards and sparkling fountains.

Each deluxe guest room at Vintners is its own private oasis with full amenities, including bathrobes, hair dryer, refrigerator, movies, whirlpool spa, and safe deposit box.

An experienced concierge will provide guests with information on wine tours in nearby Sonoma, Russian River, Dry Creek and Napa Valleys.

A perfect morning begins with a full breakfast buffet to be enjoyed either on the terrace, in the Sun Room, or by the fire in the Fireside Dining Room.

INNKEEPERS: *Don & Rhonda Carano*
ADDRESS: *4350 Barnes Road*
Santa Rosa, CA 95403
TELEPHONE: *(707) 575-7350*
E-MAIL: *info@vintnersinn.com*
WEBSITE: *www.vintnersinn.com*
ROOMS: *44 Rooms; All with private baths*
CHILDREN: *Welcome*
ANIMALS: *Prohibited; Resident cat: "Gracie"*

call first

White Chocolate Coconut Macadamia Cookies

Makes 24 large cookies.

These wonderful cookies have a macaroon-like texture—indulge and enjoy.

⅔ **cup butter or margarine**
⅔ **cup sugar**
½ **cup packed brown sugar**
1 large egg
1 teaspoon vanilla extract
1½ cups all-purpose flour
9 ounces white chocolate, chopped into ½-inch pieces
1½ cups shredded coconut
1 (3½-ounce) jar salted macadamia nuts, coarsely chopped

Preheat the oven to 325°F. Lightly grease a cookie sheet. In a large bowl, beat the butter, both sugars, egg, and vanilla with an electric mixer until fluffy. Add the flour and beat just until blended. Stir in the white chocolate, coconut, and nuts. Drop heaping tablespoonfuls of dough, at least 2 inches apart, onto the cookie sheet. Bake 17 minutes or until the edges of the cookies are lightly browned and tops look dry. Allow the cookies to cool slightly on the cookie sheet; then remove to a wire rack to cool completely. Store the cookies in an airtight container.

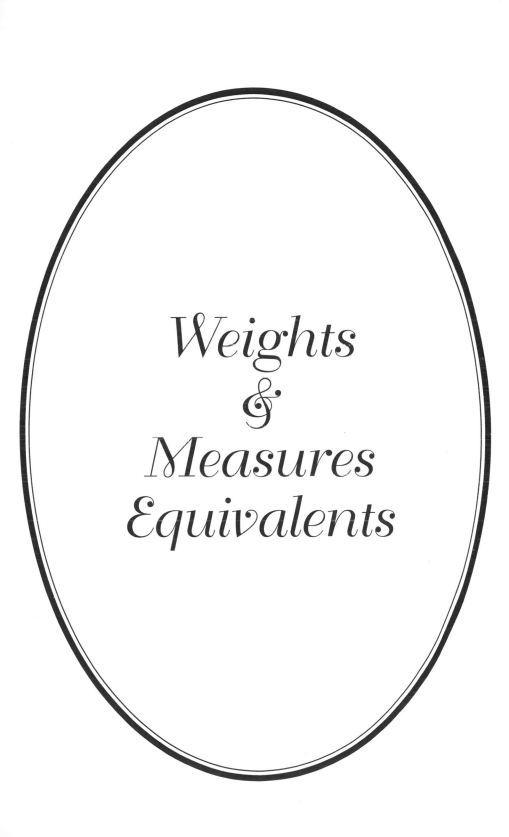

Weights
&
Measures
Equivalents

By making a few conversions, cooks not accustomed to the U.S. measurement system can still make the recipes found in this book. Use the helpful charts below and on the opposite page to find the metric equivalents.

OVEN TEMPERATURE EQUIVALENTS		
FAHRENHEIT	**CELSIUS**	**GAS SETTING**
250	120	½
275	140	1
300	150	2
325	160	3
350	180	4
375	190	5
400	200	6
425	220	7
450	230	8
475	240	9
500	260	10

BAKING PAN SIZES	
AMERICAN	**METRIC**
11x7x½-inch pan	28x18x4-centimeter pan
13x9x2-inch pan	32.5x23x5-centimeter pan
15x10x2-inch pan	38x25.5x2.5-centimeter pan
9-inch pie plate	22x4- or 23x4-centimeter pie plate
9x5x3-inch loaf pan	23x13x6-centimeter or 2-pound narrow loaf pan
1½-quart casserole	1.5-liter casserole

LENGTH MEASURES	
⅛ inch	3 millimeters
¼ inch	6 millimeters
½ inch	12 millimeters
1 inch	2.5 centimeters

LIQUID AND DRY MEASURES	
U.S.	**METRIC (ROUNDED)**
¼ teaspoon	1.25 milliliters
½ teaspoon	2.5 milliliters
1 teaspoon	5 milliliters
1 tablespoon (3 teaspoons)	15 milliliters
1 fluid ounce (2 tablespoons)	30 milliliters
¼ cup	60 milliliters
⅓ cup	80 milliliters
1 cup	240 milliliters
1 pint (2 cups)	480 milliliters
1 quart (4 cups, 32 ounces)	960 milliliters
1 gallon (4 quarts)	3.84 liters
1 ounce (by weight)	28 grams
¼ pound (4 ounces)	114 grams
1 pound	454 grams
2¼ pounds	1 kilogram

High-Altitude Adjustment Suggestions

If you live in a high-altitude region, you may find it necessary to make some minor adjustments when baking. This is due to the following facts:

- Air pressure is lower at higher altitudes, causing baked foods to rise faster.
- The atmosphere at higher altitudes is drier; consequently, flour is drier and will absorb more liquid.
- Foods take longer to cook at higher altitudes.
- Liquids evaporate more rapidly at higher altitudes.

Although there are no hard and fast rules, the following guide will help you make adjustments in your favorite cake recipes. Since every recipe is different, you may have to experiment a few times with each recipe to discover the best proportions. Start by making the first two suggested changes. If this doesn't seem to be enough, next time try another one or two suggested adjustments. With experimentation, you will become successful.

HELPFUL HINTS

Cookies: For cake-type cookies, reduce sugar by 3 tablespoons per cup. For drop cookies, test bake 2 or 3 cookies. If they flatten too much, add 2 to 4 tablespoons flour.

Pie crusts: They may require slightly more liquid but are baked at the same temperature.

Yeast breads: May require a shorter rising time and should rise only until double in size. Use slightly less flour, judging by the feel of the dough.

CAKE RECIPE HIGH ALTITUDE ADJUSTMENT GUIDE			
ADJUSTMENT	**3,000 FT.**	**5,000 FT.**	**7,000 FT.**
BAKING POWDER For each teaspoon decrease:	⅛ teaspoon	⅛ teaspoon to ¼ teaspoon	¼ teaspoon
SUGAR For each cup decrease:	1 to 2 tablespoons	2 to 4 tablespoons	3 to 4 tablespoons
FAT For each cup decrease:	1 to 2 tablespoons	2 to 4 tablespoons	3 to 4 tablespoons
LIQUID For each cup add:	1 to 2 tablespoons	2 to 4 tablespoons	3 to 4 tablespoons
TEMPERATURE Increase:	15°F	15° to 25°F	20° to 25°F

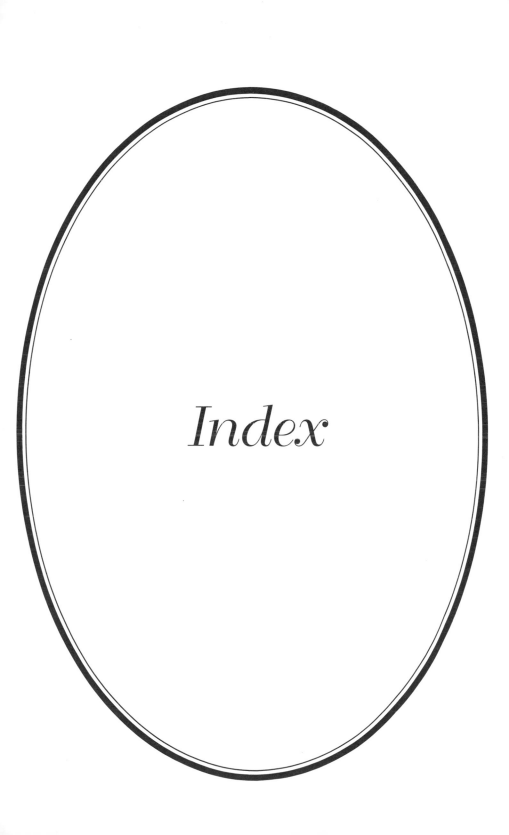

Index

Bed & Breakfast Index

Boldface indicates the page with the inn information.

Recipe Index

The Authors

Carol McCollum Faino (left) started cooking as a young girl. Her creative cooking efforts continued as she grew and were publicly recognized when she received the Home Economics Superintendent's award as a high school senior. Throughout the following years when she wasn't teaching school or raising a family, she devoted much of her time perfecting those winning skills through such varied cooking classes as Cooking with Natural Foods to Szechwan Chinese Cookery. Today, cooking is her forte. Carol tested hundreds of recipes before choosing the select recipe collection. She is also coauthor of the *Colorado Bed & Breakfast Cookbook* and the *Washington State Bed & Breakfast Cookbook*.

Doreen Kaitfors Hazledine (right) is a former Mrs. South Dakota who traveled extensively, gave inspirational speeches, and was named an Outstanding Young Woman of America. She was a teacher and businesswoman before starting a writing career. Her varied writing talents range from travel writing to inspirational nonfiction to screenwriting. A Hollywood producer optioned one of her screenplays. Doreen wrote the travel commentary. She is also coauthor of the *Colorado Bed & Breakfast Cookbook* and the *Washington State Bed & Breakfast Cookbook*.